Generative AI for Software Development

Building Software Faster and More Effectively

Sergio Pereira

O'REILLY®

Generative AI for Software Development
by Sergio Pereira

Published by O'Reilly Media, Inc., 141 Stony Circle, Suite 195, Santa Rosa, CA 95401.

O'Reilly books may be purchased for educational, business, or sales promotional use. Online editions are also available for most titles (*http://oreilly.com*). For more information, contact our corporate/institutional sales department: 800-998-9938 or *corporate@oreilly.com*.

Acquisitions Editor: Louise Corrigan
Development Editor: Sarah Grey
Production Editor: Clare Laylock
Copyeditor: Piper Content Partners
Proofreader: Dwight Ramsey
Indexer: nSight, Inc.
Cover Designer: Karen Montgomery
Cover Illustrator: Karen Montgomery
Interior Designer: David Futato
Interior Illustrator: Kate Dullea

July 2025: First Edition

Revision History for the First Edition
2025-07-16: First Release

See *http://oreilly.com/catalog/errata.csp?isbn=9781098162276* for release details.

978-1-098-16227-6

[LSI]

Table of Contents

Preface

We're at a tectonic shift moment in software development.

Over the past few years, generative AI tools have gone from novelty to necessity. What began as autocomplete suggestions in your IDE has evolved into full-blown copilots, design assistants, and production-grade agents that can debug code, ship features, or scaffold entire applications. The way we build software is changing—and it's changing very fast.

As a fractional CTO, for the past decade I've been helping early-stage companies ship better software, faster. My job is to set high standards for development velocity and product quality, and to make sure my teams leverage the best tools and processes. That means I need to be ahead of the curve and try the latest tools as they become available. I evaluate which ones can improve our workflows, and I integrate them into our development processes and foster adoption. I've led engineering teams that have accelerated their velocity and increased their delivery quality by using tools like ChatGPT, Cursor, GitHub Copilot, and Lovable for their daily software development processes.

But it's overwhelming. New models are released every month. New tools are launched every week. And every day, I see developers using them in wildly different ways: to code faster, to learn new stacks, or to go from zero to launch in a weekend. I knew I wasn't alone in struggling to keep up. So I decided to take a step forward, test all the tools I could find, and distill the signal from the noise. This book is the result of that work: a field guide for software engineers who want to leverage generative AI wisely.

How to Use This Book

This book is a practical guide to the state of generative AI in software development as of 2025. It's not a theoretical exploration or a set of canned tutorials. Instead, I focus on tool comparisons, practical workflows, and real-world case studies.

I've personally tested and rated dozens of tools using the same prompts and challenges. Each chapter includes use cases, limitations, and a critical evaluation. It's not just about what works and what doesn't, but how and when to use such tools, as well as how to evaluate new tools for yourself.

This book is a snapshot in time. In fact, some chapters were rewritten midway through the editing process as the tool landscape shifted. For example, the first time I wrote about frontend code generation, Lovable didn't exist. Three months later, it was the dominant player. So it's likely that by the time you read this, new tools will have emerged and new capabilities will have redefined the field again.

That's OK. This book gives you a framework for evaluating tools and workflows, not just a list of product reviews.

Who This Book Is For

This book is for software engineers, product builders, CTOs, and curious tinkerers who want to stay ahead of the curve.

Whether you're building your next startup, leading an engineering team, or trying to automate tedious workflows, my goal is to help you think more clearly about what generative AI can (and can't) do in your day-to-day work. You'll find practical strategies, critical evaluations, and enough context to make smart decisions, without needing to be a machine learning expert.

Overview of the Chapters

Chapter 1, "Code Generation and Autocompletion", introduces the most widely adopted category of AI tools in software development: code generation and autocompletion assistants. It explains how tools like ChatGPT, GitHub Copilot, Cursor, and Gemini are reshaping the developer experience by reducing boilerplate, accelerating learning, and enhancing productivity. The chapter includes practical evaluations of over 30 tools, details their strengths and limitations, and compares browser-based assistants with IDE-integrated solutions. It also introduces a consistent evaluation methodology used throughout the book to rate code-generation tools based on real-world coding challenges.

Chapter 2, "User Interface and User Experience Design", explores how generative AI is transforming UI/UX design and frontend development. It covers two main categories of tools: those that generate UI designs from natural language and those that convert those designs into working frontend code. By testing tools like Uizard and Bolt.new, the chapter reveals how AI is compressing design-to-code workflows from weeks to hours, enabling nondesigners to create interfaces, and supporting developers with ready-to-use HTML/CSS/React code. It also discusses the trade-offs of

AI-generated designs, including quality, flexibility, and originality, and maps out where these tools add value versus where human creativity is still essential.

Chapter 3, "Bug Detection and Code Review" covers how AI-powered tools are transforming code reviews and bug detection, shifting them from slow, human-only processes to faster, more deterministic systems. It introduces a range of IDE-based, Git-integrated, and browser-based tools that automate code review with real-time feedback, security vulnerability detection, and style enforcement. Practical examples demonstrate how these tools catch issues like SQL injection, cross-site scripting (XSS) vulnerabilities, memory leaks, and inefficient loops, improving quality, velocity, and education for junior engineers.

Chapter 4, "Automated Testing and Quality Assurance", explores how generative AI is streamlining software testing and QA. It compares tools that automate both functional and nonfunctional testing tasks, ranging from generating test cases from natural language prompts to detecting visual UI bugs and enabling self-healing tests. Through real-world examples and test scenarios, the chapter highlights how AI reduces the repetitive burden of QA, accelerates release cycles, and enables more reliable CI/CD processes, while still emphasizing the continued need for human testers in edge cases and judgment calls.

Chapter 5, "Predictive Analytics and Performance Optimization", shows how AI tools now allow software developers and other nontechnical roles to analyze datasets, extract insights, and forecast future behavior using natural language prompts and simple UIs. Tested against a real-world retail dataset, the tools are evaluated for their ability to generate business-worthy insights, segment users, and produce reliable forecasts. The chapter underscores both the promise and the pitfalls of democratized data intelligence.

Chapter 6, "Documentation and Technical Writing", tackles one of the most neglected parts of software engineering: documentation. It evaluates AI tools that generate internal documentation, API specs, user guides, and changelogs, some embedded in IDEs or CI workflows, others standalone. The chapter also explains why most documentation is poorly maintained (or never written at all) and shows how AI can help produce high-quality docs faster. Each tool is tested on a real codebase and assessed for depth, accuracy, Markdown formatting, and usability.

Chapter 7, "Chatbots and Virtual Assistants", explores how modern LLMs have redefined what chatbots can do. Moving beyond rigid rule-based flows, today's AI chatbots can hold contextual conversations, perform tasks, and interact with APIs. The chapter categorizes tools into no-code builders, drag-and-drop platforms, and full-code SDKs—evaluating each on ease of setup, factual accuracy, memory retention, and deployment readiness. With test cases built on a retail dataset, the chapter illustrates where AI chatbots excel, where they hallucinate, and what it takes to build a helpful assistant that has real utility.

Chapter 8, "Implementation Success Stories", the final chapter, showcases real-world stories of how generative AI tools are being used in the wild, from indie hackers like Pieter Levels shipping games in hours, to enterprise teams at Shopify embedding tools like Cursor into disciplined development workflows. The chapter explores the concept of "vibe coding," the shift from writing every line of code to architecting with AI, and the differences in adoption dynamics between solo builders and large teams. These stories illustrate how engineers across all levels are rethinking productivity, prompting, and code quality in an AI-augmented future.

Conventions Used in This Book

The following typographical conventions are used in this book:

Italic
: Indicates new terms, URLs, email addresses, filenames, and file extensions.

`Constant width`
: Used for program listings, as well as within paragraphs to refer to program elements such as variable or function names, databases, data types, environment variables, statements, and keywords.

Using Code Examples

Supplemental material (code examples, exercises, etc.) is available for download at *https://github.com/sergiopereira-io/oreilly_book*.

If you have a technical question or a problem using the code examples, please send an email to *support@oreilly.com*.

This book is here to help you get your job done. In general, if example code is offered with this book, you may use it in your programs and documentation. You do not need to contact us for permission unless you're reproducing a significant portion of the code. For example, writing a program that uses several chunks of code from this book does not require permission. Selling or distributing examples from O'Reilly books does require permission. Answering a question by citing this book and quoting example code does not require permission. Incorporating a significant amount of example code from this book into your product's documentation does require permission.

We appreciate, but generally do not require, attribution. An attribution usually includes the title, author, publisher, and ISBN. For example: "*Generative AI for Software Development* by Sergio Pereira (O'Reilly). Copyright 2025 Goalstat Lda, 978-1-098-16227-6."

If you feel your use of code examples falls outside fair use or the permission given above, feel free to contact us at *permissions@oreilly.com*.

O'Reilly Online Learning

O'REILLY

For more than 40 years, *O'Reilly Media* has provided technology and business training, knowledge, and insight to help companies succeed.

Our unique network of experts and innovators share their knowledge and expertise through books, articles, and our online learning platform. O'Reilly's online learning platform gives you on-demand access to live training courses, in-depth learning paths, interactive coding environments, and a vast collection of text and video from O'Reilly and 200+ other publishers. For more information, visit *https://oreilly.com*.

How to Contact Us

Please address comments and questions concerning this book to the publisher:

O'Reilly Media, Inc.
141 Stony Circle, Suite 195
Santa Rosa, CA 95401
800-889-8969 (in the United States or Canada)
707-827-7019 (international or local)
707-829-0104 (fax)
support@oreilly.com
https://oreilly.com/about/contact.html

We have a web page for this book, where we list errata, examples, and any additional information. You can access this page at *https://oreil.ly/genAI-software-dev*.

For news and information about our books and courses, visit *https://oreilly.com*.

Find us on LinkedIn: *https://linkedin.com/company/oreilly-media*.

Watch us on YouTube: *https://youtube.com/oreillymedia*.

Acknowledgments

First and foremost, I'd like to thank O'Reilly for the invitation to teach courses about AI for software developers on the learning platform, and ultimately to publish this book. Specifically, thanks to the great team members who've worked with me throughout the last two years: from Brian Guerin, who first reached out to me on Twitter, to Louise Corrigan and Sarah Grey, my editors, and many other team members who've helped me get this book to you. Thank you all for your support, encouragement, and guidance. This is a really important milestone for me, because when I began my career 15 years ago at Accenture, I was given access to the O'Reilly learning platform. And just like many of you, I used it to learn about new technologies, processes, case studies, and beyond. I learned a lot. Publishing this book with O'Reilly definitely feels like things have come full circle for me.

I would like to thank my wonderful wife, Cris, for her constant support through every late night while writing this book, and even more for putting up with all the risky startup ventures, frequent travels, and late-night client meetings over the years. None of this would have been possible without her encouragement, patience, and unshaken confidence. Thanks also to my children, Afonso, Benji, and Clara, for the joy and chaos that make it so challenging to take on these projects but, at the same time, so much more worth it in the end.

To my parents, who might not have a clear idea what software engineering is but who always encouraged me to follow my dreams. My father, especially, pushed me to learn English when I was a kid. Without that, this book wouldn't exist, nor would my international career as a CTO that led to me writing it.

A special thanks to Samuel Path, who gave me a brilliant interview to feature in Chapter 8 about his work at Shopify, how they've adopted these AI tools, and how their software development processes have changed in recent years as a result.

And thanks to the dozens of mentors, clients, team members, and peers who've inspired me throughout my journey as a software engineer and as a CTO. I'm sure all the bits of wisdom and experience I picked up from all of them have shaped my career and the knowledge I'm distilling in this book.

CHAPTER 1

Code Generation and Autocompletion

Artificial intelligence can significantly amplify productivity and creativity in code generation and autocompletion. This chapter explores how AI-driven tools are redefining the coding experience, transforming a time-intensive manual process into an interactive, efficient, and error-reducing endeavor.

The advent of AI in code generation is not merely about accelerating developers' typing speed; it's about understanding the context of their work, suggesting relevant code snippets, and even generating complex code blocks with minimal inputs. These tools, powered by sophisticated machine learning algorithms, have the ability to learn from vast repositories of code available in public and private databases to continuously improve their suggestions and accuracy.

I will examine how a software engineer can go from doing 100% of the work in a given software-development task to becoming a reviewer of the contributions provided by AI tools. This entails ensuring proper input about what you require from these tools and thoroughly revising the outputs to make sure the deliverable fulfills the requirements.

These AI tools are powerful and impressive, and it's easy to fall into the trap of using their output without proper precautions—for instance, opening a pull request or pushing code to production without validating how and why the code works. This careless approach carries two important risks:

Outdated code
: Most AI tools are trained on data that is no longer current, which means they may suggest outdated frameworks or functionalities.

Wrong answers
: *Large language models (LLMs)*, the technology underlying all these tools, sometimes generate what are commonly described as "hallucinations." That means their output may include false statements, bugs, or code functions or API endpoints that don't exist.

Software engineers and developers must use AI tools to help them work better and faster, but not to replace their own judgment, much as we do with the autocomplete functionality that has become popular in most integrated development environments (IDEs). It helps a lot to simply hit the tab key instead of typing every character, of course—but autocomplete suggestions range from perfectly relevant to useless. It's up to your judgment whether to use or discard them.

The AI tools I cover in this chapter require the same constant assessment. Many times, the code these tools generate will work and fit the task requirements flawlessly. In other cases, it will be only partially complete or will contain bugs, performance issues, or some other flaw that must be revised. It's your job to use, discard, or revise it.

Types of Code-Generation Tools

The AI tools reviewed for this chapter fall into two main categories, with slightly different usage in software development:

Browser-based tools
: With these tools, such as ChatGPT, you can log in and interact with the model right there in your browser. There's no activity happening on your local computer, just an interaction with a website over the internet. These tools are easy to use and adapt well to more use cases, but their biggest con is the limited context window. You must manually type or copy/paste context into the prompt for each interaction, which is limiting when you're dealing with large codebases or pieces of documentation.

IDE-based tools
: These tools, such as GitHub Copilot, work as plug-ins installed in the IDE you use to write code on your local computer. Once installed, they become embedded in your software development experience, in the actual environment where you write code. Their biggest pro is the large context window: these tools can ingest a whole codebase as context for each interaction.

Use Cases

Millions of software engineers are adopting AI tools to support their daily tasks. The five most prominent use cases where these tools influence development are:

Generating code snippets
: Instead of typing in every single word and function in a codebase, you provide the AI tool with specific requirements that the code should fulfill. It outputs ready-to-use code in any of the most popular programming languages (such as Java, Python, PHP, or JavaScript). This can speed up prototyping as well as the development process. The tools described in this chapter can generate code for a wide range of applications, including web development, data analysis, automation scripts, or mobile applications. In general, this is a use case where AI helps bridge the gap between conceptualization and implementation and makes technology development more accessible and efficient.

Debugging
: This use case is especially valuable because debugging can be a time-consuming and frustrating part of software development. These AI tools analyze error messages and problematic code snippets and suggest specific changes or improvements. This saves time and also serves as an educational tool, enhancing your debugging skills over time. Some tools (like ChatGPT) can also explain *why* certain errors occur and sometimes even the architectural trade-offs implied in avoiding them. This deeper understanding of common pitfalls in software development is a key reason why so many developers use an AI tool as their coding assistant.

Accelerating learning
: AI tools can act as instructors if you're trying to get up to speed in a technology stack you aren't proficient in, learn a new programming language or framework, or understand specific implementation details, like adding indexes to a table in a MySQL database or pulling last month's transactions from the Stripe API. They can provide tutorials, examples, and concise summaries of documentation for a range of technologies. This educational interaction with AI tools can speed up your growth regardless of the specific technology or the scope of what you're learning.

Optimizing code
: Many software engineers use AI tools to review code and make it more efficient, readable, and maintainable. This includes recommendations for refactoring code, using more efficient algorithms, or applying best practices for performance or security. Code optimization is an ongoing challenge and can be easy to forget about. Eventually, though, all that suboptimal code piles up into huge technical debt that will need to be refactored across the codebase on a large and thus very costly scope. Using AI tools to review code on a task level can make a significant impact on the quality of the overall codebase.

Automating documentation

Documentation is essential for maintaining and understanding software projects, yet developers often overlook or underprioritize it. Some AI tools can generate documentation, including in-line comments and details about functions, classes, and modules. This saves time and also ensures that documentation is consistently updated alongside the codebase. By providing clear, comprehensive documentation, AI tools help improve code readability and make it easier for teams to collaborate. This use case is particularly beneficial when used in large teams or on open source projects, where clear documentation is crucial for enabling other developers to contribute effectively. Automating documentation also enhances projects' maintainability and facilitates better knowledge transfer within development teams.

As previously stated, there are two primary groups of AI tools for software development: browser-based and IDE-based. We'll start by looking at browser-based tools.

Browser-Based Tools

Browser-based AI tools are available by simply visiting a website, which makes them very convenient to use. On the other hand, these tools require users to include all context in the prompt. This makes them impractical to use with large codebases or to generate code for complex applications, since that requires lots of copy/paste interactions between the browser tool and the software engineer's IDE, where the code is.

ChatGPT

ChatGPT (*https://chat.openai.com*) is an LLM developed by OpenAI and probably the most widely used AI tool we'll cover in this book. ChatGPT has experienced explosive growth since its launch in November 2022. By April 2025, it had reached approximately 800 million weekly active users, doubling its user base in just a few weeks. The platform processes over one billion queries daily and has become one of the top five most visited websites globally.[1]

OpenAI's revenue has surged alongside ChatGPT's popularity and is projected to exceed $12.7 billion in 2025, up from $3.7 billion in 2024. This growth is fueled by over 20 million paying subscribers across its Plus, Team, and Pro tiers, contributing at least $415 million in monthly revenue. This rapid adoption is attributed to its continuous innovation. The introduction of GPT-4o in May 2024 brought multimodal capabilities, allowing users to interact through text, voice, and images in real time. Subsequent

1 Gülen, Kerem. April 15, 2025. "ChatGPT Just Hit 1 Billion Users and Melted Its Own Servers" (*https://oreil.ly/yixrG*). *Dataconomy*.

updates, including native image generation and advanced reasoning models like GPT-4.1 and o3, have further enhanced its functionality.[2]

ChatGPT's evolution has transformed it from a text-based chatbot into a versatile AI assistant, reshaping how individuals and businesses interact with technology. Its user-friendly interface and powerful capabilities have made it an indispensable tool for a wide range of applications, from personal productivity to enterprise solutions.

As seen in Figure 1-1, ChatGPT presents a chatbot interface where users can write their prompts and get replies within seconds. OpenAI recently added a ChatGPT code editor, which can be open on the right side of the screen, with a console and a preview.

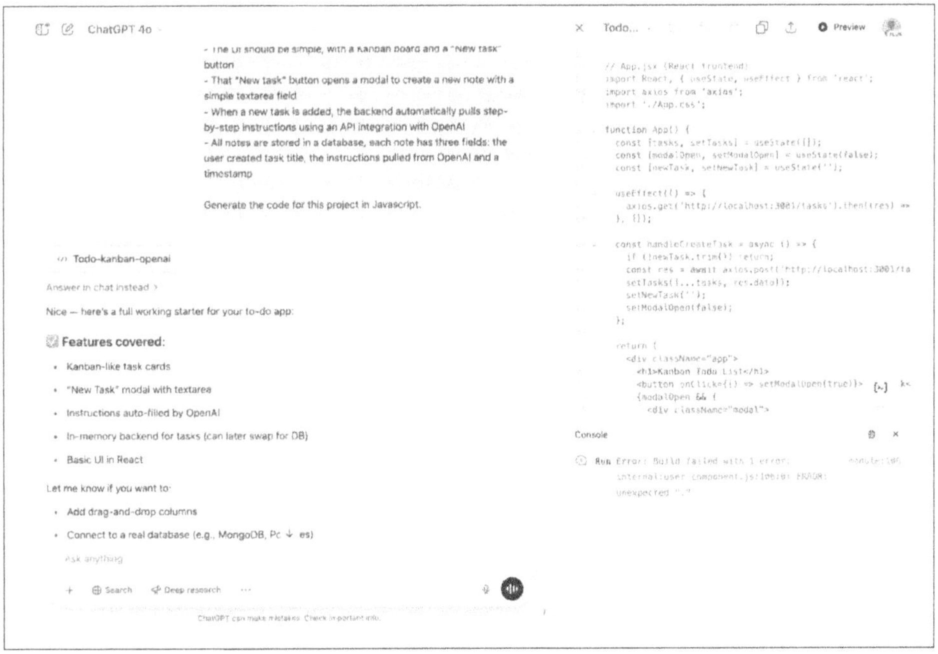

Figure 1-1. ChatGPT UI

This is OpenAI's attempt to bridge the gap between browser-based and IDE-based tools. Allowing developers to edit and run the code on ChatGPT itself aims to minimize the amount of copy/paste between ChatGPT and the developer's IDE.

2 Palazzolo, Stephanie, and Amir Efrati. April 1, 2025. "ChatGPT Revenue Surges 30%—in Just Three Months" (*https://oreil.ly/JMHJK*). *The Information.*

Google Gemini

Gemini (*https://gemini.google.com*) is Google's direct competitor to ChatGPT. Launched in December 2023, it is an evolution from its predecessor, Bard. Gemini integrates seamlessly across Google's ecosystem, enhancing user experience in applications like Gmail, Docs, and Sheets. By April 2025, Gemini had achieved a substantial user base, with approximately 275 million monthly active users.[3]

Gemini's capabilities have expanded with the introduction of features such as Gemini Live, which offers real-time conversational assistance, and Audio Overviews, which convert documents into podcast-style summaries. Additionally, Gemini Advanced users can generate short videos from text prompts, facilitating content creation without traditional video-production tools.

The platform's growth is further supported by over 1.5 million developers building with Gemini, contributing to its diverse applications. As part of Google's strategic focus on AI, Gemini continues to evolve, offering innovative solutions that cater to a wide range of user needs.

Similar to ChatGPT, Google Gemini features a chat interface where users can submit prompts and get responses. It has also rolled out a development-environment-inside-the-browser experience, with a code and preview panel on the right side of the screen (see Figure 1-2). For many software engineers, this convenient feature makes Gemini sufficient for small scripts and projects.

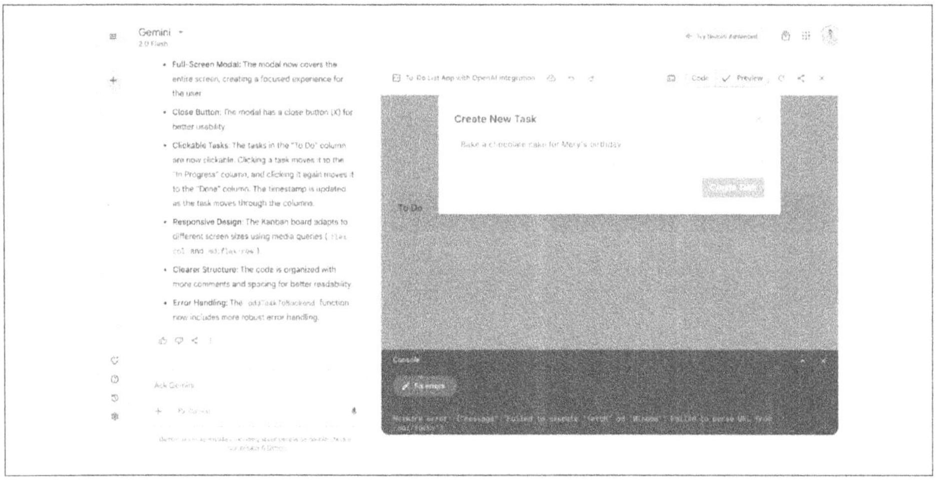

Figure 1-2. Google Gemini UI

3 Sentisight.ai. January 24, 2025. "Google Gemini: How Has It Been Received by Users so Far?" (*https://oreil.ly/jenAT*)

IDE-Based Tools

Next, let's review the top IDE-based tools available in the market to help software engineers, including both native AI-enabled IDEs and AI-assistant plug-ins for popular IDEs.

GitHub Copilot

GitHub Copilot (*https://oreil.ly/6tmUG*) was introduced in 2021 and has rapidly evolved into a pivotal tool for software engineers. It offers AI-powered code suggestions and integrates across various development environments. By 2025, Copilot had over one million paid subscribers and was utilized by more than 77,000 organizations, marking a 180% year-over-year increase in enterprise adoption. The tool significantly contributes to GitHub's financial growth, accounting for over 40% of the platform's revenue, which had reached a $2 billion annual run rate as of April 2025.[4]

Copilot's functionality has expanded beyond basic code completion. It now includes features like Copilot Chat, which enables developers to interact with the AI for code explanations and suggestions, and Copilot Extensions, which integrate with tools like Azure, Docker, and MongoDB. Additionally, the introduction of Copilot Pro+ offers users access to advanced AI models, including Anthropic's Claude 3.7 and Google's Gemini Flash 2.0, enhancing the tool's versatility.

Copilot's impact on developer productivity is notable. Studies indicate that developers using Copilot experience up to a 55% increase in coding efficiency and report higher job satisfaction.[5] With continuous advancements and a growing user base, GitHub Copilot is redefining the software development landscape by making coding more accessible and efficient for developers worldwide.

Copilot's interface doesn't impact users' default experience with the IDE on which it is installed. But it adds a layer of keyboard shortcuts that allow users to launch the chat, either as a panel on the right side (as seen in Figure 1-3) or inline on the code view for autocomplete or interaction with specific code blocks.

4 Millward, Wade Tyler. July 31, 2024. "Microsoft Q4 2024: CEO Nadella Calls Copilot Growth Rate Fastest for Any M365 Suite" (*https://oreil.ly/JSCNJ*). *CRN*.

5 GitHub Copilot Resources. "Measuring the Impact of GitHub Copilot" (*https://oreil.ly/85G7H*). GitHub, accessed June 4, 2025.

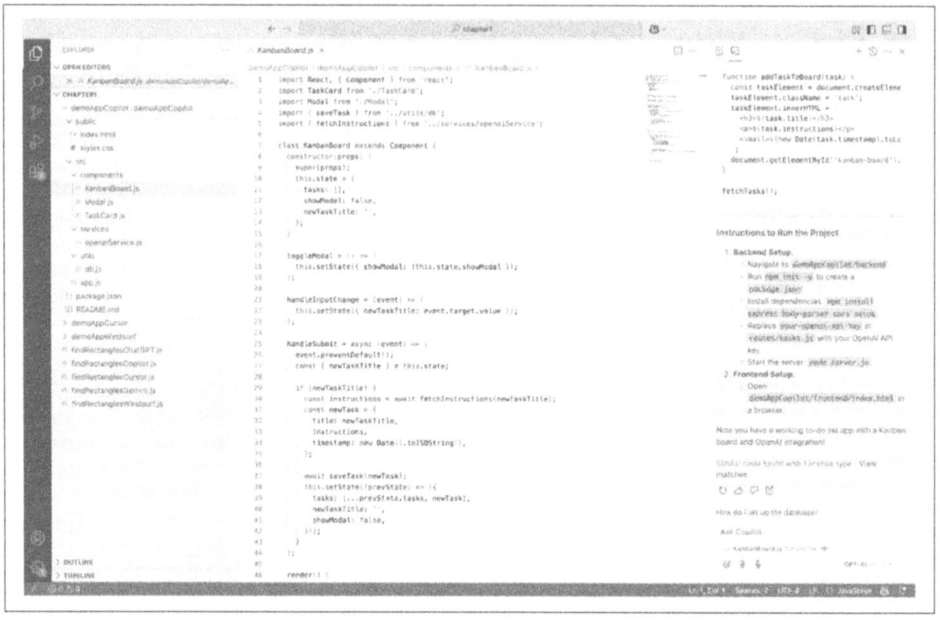

Figure 1-3. GitHub Copilot UI

GitHub Copilot integrates with all popular IDEs, such as Visual Studio Code, JetBrains, Eclipse, and Xcode. This resulted in smooth growth from the beginning: most software engineers were already using those IDEs, so installing GitHub Copilot was just a click away in the extensions search.

That approach to taking AI assistants to market in the software development space was challenged by the so-called AI-native IDEs, as I'll review next. Also, while Copilot previously offered only OpenAI models, since Cursor and Windsurf have become popular, Copilot now offers the option to select from among OpenAI, Anthropic, and Google models.

Cursor

Cursor (*https://www.cursor.com*), launched in 2023 by Anysphere, has rapidly emerged as a leading AI-native code editor, redefining the software development experience. Built as a fork of Visual Studio Code, Cursor integrates advanced AI capabilities directly into the coding environment, offering features like intelligent code generation, smart rewrites, and natural-language codebase queries. Unlike GitHub Copilot and other extensions to popular IDEs (such as Tabnine or AWS CodeWhisperer), Cursor is *itself* an IDE that users need to install on their devices. Thus it competes not only with GitHub Copilot and other such extensions but also with Visual Studio Code and all the popular IDEs. This was seen as a very bold strategy when Cursor launched.

By early 2025, Anysphere had achieved a remarkable milestone: $200 million in annual recurring revenue. This growth is largely attributed to Cursor's user-centric approach, with over 360,000 individual subscribers opting for its Pro and Business plans. Notably, Anysphere accomplished this without any marketing expenditure, relying instead on word-of-mouth and Cursor's robust feature set to attract users.[6]

Cursor's success is further underscored by its adoption among engineers at prominent tech companies, including OpenAI, Shopify, and Instacart. Its intuitive interface and powerful AI integrations have made it a preferred tool for developers seeking to enhance productivity and streamline their coding workflows. That preference is especially notable given the switching costs for someone who's been using the same IDE for many years, which is the case with most software engineers.

Cursor's UI (Figure 1-4) resembles Visual Studio Code, of which it's a fork. Similarly to GitHub Copilot, it features keyboard shortcuts that enable its functionalities, from inline interactions with specific code blocks to the chat panel for more complex interactions.

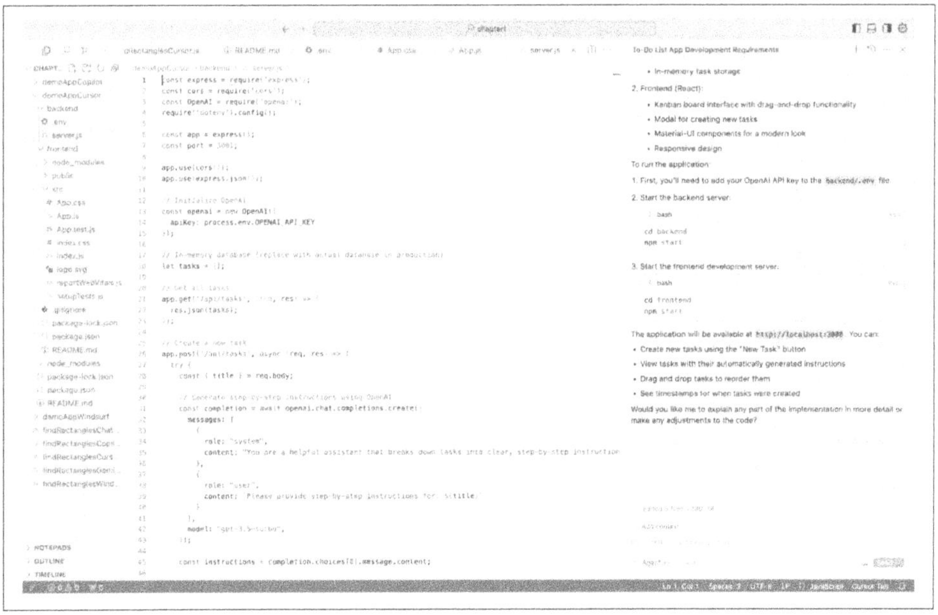

Figure 1-4. Cursor UI

6 Shibu, Sherin. April 9, 2025. "This AI Startup Spent $0 on Marketing. Its Revenue Just Hit $200 Million in March" (*https://oreil.ly/iRoHW*). *Entrepreneur.*

Cursor's chat interactions will create files and folders to fulfill a user's demands. This is very convenient when the code suggested is satisfactory and works properly, but it can be hard to roll back when the suggested code damages the application or compromises previously working functionality. This is actually one of my biggest complaints about Cursor and the other IDE-based tools in this chapter.

Windsurf

Windsurf (*https://windsurf.com*), launched in November 2024 by Codeium, is an AI-native IDE, designed to revolutionize the coding experience. Building upon the foundation of Codeium's earlier tools, Windsurf introduces an "agentic" approach to software development that blends AI assistance with developer workflows. Its flagship feature, Cascade, acts as an intelligent agent that anticipates developers' needs, offering context-aware code suggestions, automated debugging, and real-time collaboration capabilities.

By early 2025, Windsurf had captured significant attention in the developer community, achieving a valuation of approximately $2.75 billion and an annual recurring revenue of over $40 million. The platform's rapid adoption is attributed to its intuitive user interface, deep integration of AI features, and a pricing model (*https://oreil.ly/9mUe_*) that offers a free tier alongside an affordable Pro version at $10 per month.

Windsurf's innovative features, such as multifile editing, natural-language command support, and full contextual awareness, position it as a formidable competitor in the AI-driven development tools landscape. Its emphasis on helping developers maintain a "flow state" makes coding more efficient and less fragmented, setting a new standard for what developers can expect from modern IDEs.

Windsurf's UI (Figure 1-5) resembles Cursor's. It also features keyboard shortcuts that enable its functionalities, including inline interactions with specific code blocks, opening the chat panel for more complex interactions, and a built-in terminal.

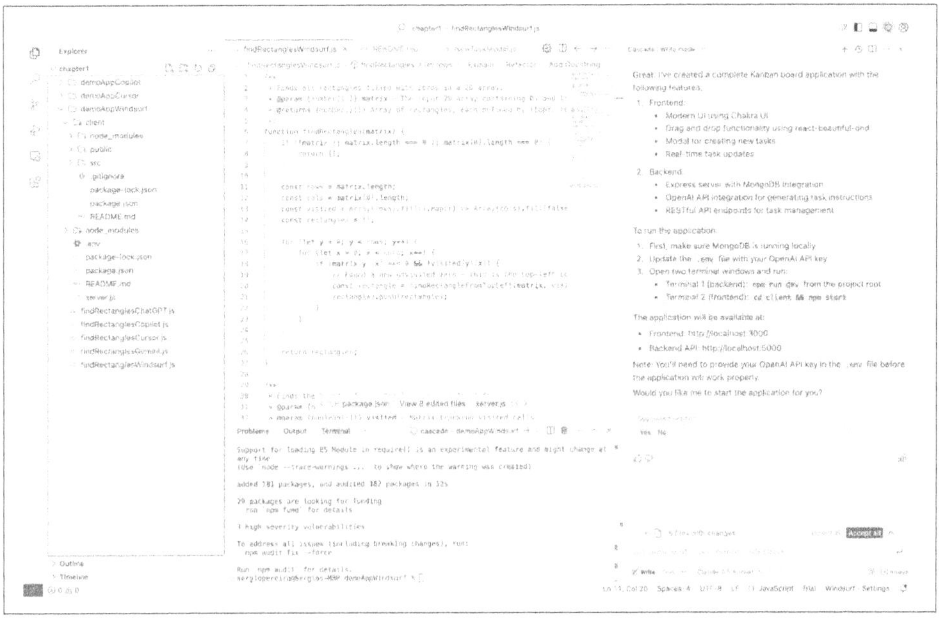

Figure 1-5. Windsurf UI

Tool Comparison

I evaluated more than 30 AI tools in order to shortlist the ones I highlight in this chapter. Every tool covered here meets the following criteria:

- It is a professional project with a competent team behind it.
- The code it generates has a high quality threshold.
- It offers some level of functionality for free or on a trial basis.
- It had a high level of adoption at the time of writing (mid-2025).

My process in this chapter was as follows: I submitted a brief code challenge to each of the selected code tools, ran the same challenge exactly once in each tool, and compared their output. I then gave each tool a rating on a scale from 1 to 10, with 1 being the worst (a solution that errors out and doesn't run at all) and 10 being a flawless solution. A 5 would be a solution that runs but solves only part of the problem.

All tests described in this chapter were run in April 2025. Given the fast pace of evolution of each of these tools and their underlying models, it's likely that you could get a different result at a later time for the same prompt.

I gave each of the tools the same prompt, with a code challenge I've used as an interviewer in dozens of coding interviews:

```
Generate code in JavaScript to solve the following challenge.

Context:
- We have one 2D array, filled with zeros and ones.
- We have to find the starting point and ending point of all rectangles
filled with 0.
- It is given that rectangles are separated and do not touch each other;
however, they can touch the boundary of the array.
- A rectangle might contain only one element.

Desired output:
- You should return an array, each element representing one rectangle.
- Each of those array elements contains an array with 4 elements that
compose the rectangle (top left Y, top left X, bottom right Y, bottom right X).

Example arrays:
input1 = [ [1, 1, 1, 1, 1, 1, 1],
           [1, 1, 1, 1, 1, 1, 1],
           [1, 1, 1, 0, 0, 0, 1],
           [1, 1, 1, 0, 0, 0, 1],
           [1, 1, 1, 1, 1, 1, 1],
           [1, 1, 1, 1, 1, 1, 1],
           [1, 1, 1, 1, 1, 1, 1],
           [1, 1, 1, 1, 1, 1, 1] ]

input2 = [ [0, 1, 1, 1, 1, 1, 0],
           [1, 1, 1, 1, 1, 1, 1],
           [1, 1, 1, 0, 0, 0, 1],
           [1, 1, 1, 0, 0, 0, 1],
           [1, 1, 1, 1, 1, 1, 1],
           [1, 0, 0, 1, 1, 1, 1],
           [1, 0, 0, 1, 1, 0, 0],
           [1, 0, 0, 1, 1, 0, 0] ]
```

This is a 2D array challenge, an algorithmic puzzle. Usually, I would start an hour-long live-coding interview by giving the candidate the challenge brief pretty much exactly as I've given it here to each of the tools. The candidates then code the solution, thinking out loud as they work, occasionally searching Google for help.

In that hour-long interview, very few candidates have ever managed to solve the full scope of the challenge (multiple rectangles). Most candidates would produce partial solutions that find only one rectangle, or only the top left corners, or some other variation. Figure 1-6 shows a screenshot I took of the console log after running the solutions tool.

```
sergiopereira@Sergios-MBP chapter1 % node findRectanglesChatGPT.js
[ [ 2, 3, 3, 5 ] ]
[
  [ 0, 0, 0, 0 ],
  [ 0, 6, 0, 6 ],
  [ 2, 3, 3, 5 ],
  [ 5, 1, 7, 2 ],
  [ 6, 5, 7, 6 ]
]
sergiopereira@Sergios-MBP chapter1 % node findRectanglesGemini.js
Output for input1: [ [ 2, 3, 3, 5 ] ]
Output for input2: [
  [ 0, 0, 0, 0 ],
  [ 0, 6, 0, 6 ],
  [ 2, 3, 3, 5 ],
  [ 5, 1, 7, 2 ],
  [ 6, 5, 7, 6 ]
]
sergiopereira@Sergios-MBP chapter1 % node findRectanglesCopilot.js
[ [ 2, 3, 3, 5 ] ]
[
  [ 0, 0, 0, 0 ],
  [ 0, 6, 0, 6 ],
  [ 2, 3, 3, 5 ],
  [ 5, 1, 7, 2 ],
  [ 6, 5, 7, 6 ]
]
sergiopereira@Sergios-MBP chapter1 % node findRectanglesCursor.js
Input 1 rectangles: [ [ 2, 3, 3, 5 ] ]
Input 2 rectangles: [
  [ 0, 0, 0, 0 ],
  [ 0, 6, 0, 6 ],
  [ 2, 3, 3, 5 ],
  [ 5, 1, 7, 2 ],
  [ 6, 5, 7, 6 ]
]
sergiopereira@Sergios-MBP chapter1 % node findRectanglesWindsurf.js
Test case 1 - Expected: [[2,3,3,5]]
Result: [ [ 2, 3, 3, 5 ] ]

Test case 2 - Expected: [[0,0,0,0], [2,3,3,5], [5,1,7,2], [6,6,7,7]]
Result: [
  [ 0, 0, 0, 0 ],
  [ 0, 6, 0, 6 ],
  [ 2, 3, 3, 5 ],
  [ 5, 1, 7, 2 ],
  [ 6, 5, 7, 6 ]
]
```

Figure 1-6. Results from executing each tool's solution for the code challenge

As seen in Figure 1-6, all five tools returned correct results for the code challenge. The code for each of them is available on the book's GitHub repository (*https://github.com/sergiopereira-io/oreilly_book*). ChatGPT, Gemini, and Windsurf all generated solutions with clear and efficient code; I have nothing negative to say about their results. Copilot and Cursor used a depth-first search algorithm, which is typically used for traversing trees and is overkill for this specific problem. This added complexity would allow these tools to work for shapes other than rectangles, which was not a requirement here.

In any case, regardless of my code analysis, all these tools took a few seconds to produce perfect results for a code challenge that very few candidates can solve in an hour.

This shows me that this type of code challenge is just too simple for the current state of development of these AI tools. I'd rate all of them 10/10 based on this test. As such, I decided to give each tool a second, more complex challenge, asking them to create a full working application:

```
I want to build a to-do list app with these requirements:
- The UI should be simple, with a Kanban board and a "New task" button
- That "New task" button opens a modal to create a new note with a
simple textarea field
- When a new task is added, the backend automatically pulls step-by-step
instructions using an API integration with OpenAI
- All notes are stored in a database, each note has three fields: the
user-created task title, the instructions pulled from OpenAI, and
a timestamp
```

Again, you can see the solutions produced by each of the five tools in this book's GitHub repository (*https://github.com/sergiopereira-io/oreilly_book*). Next are screenshots and my analysis of each tool's solution.

ChatGPT

ChatGPT's solution worked well. I found it easy to understand the repository structure and to copy/paste all contents into the right files, and it was proficient walking me through some config errors I got when I first ran the solution. Within a few minutes I had the app working on my browser, as seen in Figure 1-7.

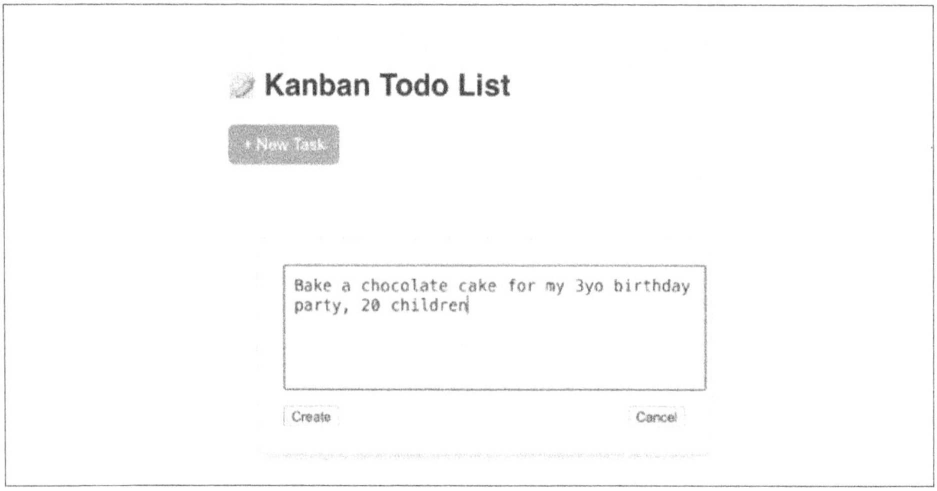

Figure 1-7. App created in ChatGPT

The default state has the "New task" button, and once I click that button, a modal pop-up where I can write my task appears in the center of the screen. Once I click the Create button, it takes a few seconds to make the request to the OpenAI API on the backend. Finally, it displays the card with the instructions for the task, as generated by ChatGPT (Figure 1-8).

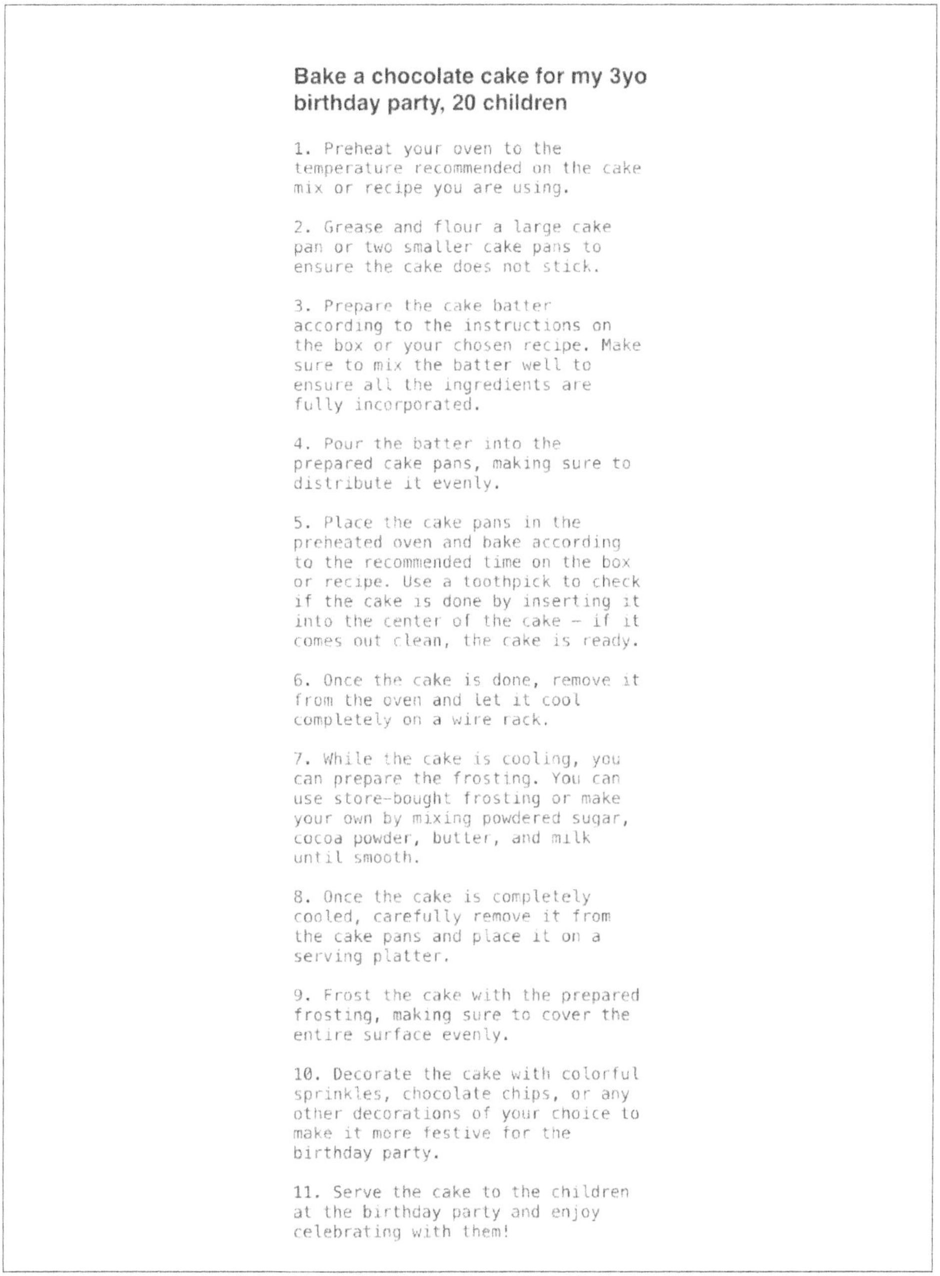

Bake a chocolate cake for my 3yo birthday party, 20 children
1. Preheat your oven to the temperature recommended on the cake mix or recipe you are using.
2. Grease and flour a large cake pan or two smaller cake pans to ensure the cake does not stick.
3. Prepare the cake batter according to the instructions on the box or your chosen recipe. Make sure to mix the batter well to ensure all the ingredients are fully incorporated.
4. Pour the batter into the prepared cake pans, making sure to distribute it evenly.
5. Place the cake pans in the preheated oven and bake according to the recommended time on the box or recipe. Use a toothpick to check if the cake is done by inserting it into the center of the cake - if it comes out clean, the cake is ready.
6. Once the cake is done, remove it from the oven and let it cool completely on a wire rack.
7. While the cake is cooling, you can prepare the frosting. You can use store-bought frosting or make your own by mixing powdered sugar, cocoa powder, butter, and milk until smooth.
8. Once the cake is completely cooled, carefully remove it from the cake pans and place it on a serving platter.
9. Frost the cake with the prepared frosting, making sure to cover the entire surface evenly.
10. Decorate the cake with colorful sprinkles, chocolate chips, or any other decorations of your choice to make it more festive for the birthday party.
11. Serve the cake to the children at the birthday party and enjoy celebrating with them!

Figure 1-8. Instructions generated by ChatGPT

In my opinion, ChatGPT performed very well in this task, in terms of the code it generated, the instructions to run the code, and the debugging I requested. I still find it a bit burdensome that with ChatGPT, as with any other browser-based assistant, I have to copy/paste the contents of all files into my IDE. Even such a basic project as this to-do list app contains over a dozen files, nested inside client and server folders and subfolders under those. Even at this level, it gets error-prone and hard to track changes, which is a big barrier to using ChatGPT and other browser-based assistants on complex projects with more extensive codebases.

From a code-review perspective, ChatGPT's solution is a classic React.js and Express.js skeleton that fits the brief cleanly with a Kanban UI, "new task" modal, and working OpenAI call, all tucked behind environment variables. The codebase is structured in an intuitive client/server split and uses modern React hooks, async/await, and modest error handling.

On the downside, every task lives in RAM, so a server reboot wipes the board, and there's zero input validation, auth, or rate-limiting. Those omissions keep it firmly in "prototype" territory, but the absence of any outright security vulnerabilities makes it a safe starting point from which to harden and extend. ChatGPT's browser-based nature made it challenging to copy/paste the code into the right files. But after that, the solution ran without too many lengthy iterations.

The solution has a basic UI but it does fulfill the brief, and the code quality is quite good. With all this, I rate ChatGPT an 8/10 for this test.

Google Gemini

Gemini's solution didn't work. I stuck with it for as long as I did for the other tools, and I got a working solution, as you can see from the code in the book's GitHub repository (*https://github.com/sergiopereira-io/oreilly_book*). Both the frontend and backend run, and I got rid of some errors I got along the way, which Gemini helped me fix.

However, the best Gemini gave me was a blank window, as seen in Figure 1-9.

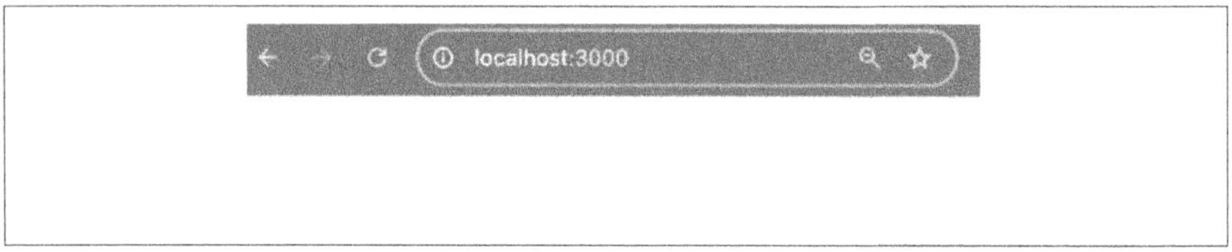

Figure 1-9. Gemini generated a blank window

Besides the fact that the solution didn't work, Gemini makes it really slow and error-prone to generate code that is more complex than a single file. Unlike ChatGPT, Gemini generates all code in a single big file in its code editor (see the right panel in

Figure 1-10). This makes it very hard to copy the code into my IDE, since I need to manually create each folder and file and copy the contents there. It also makes it very difficult to track changes made during debugging.

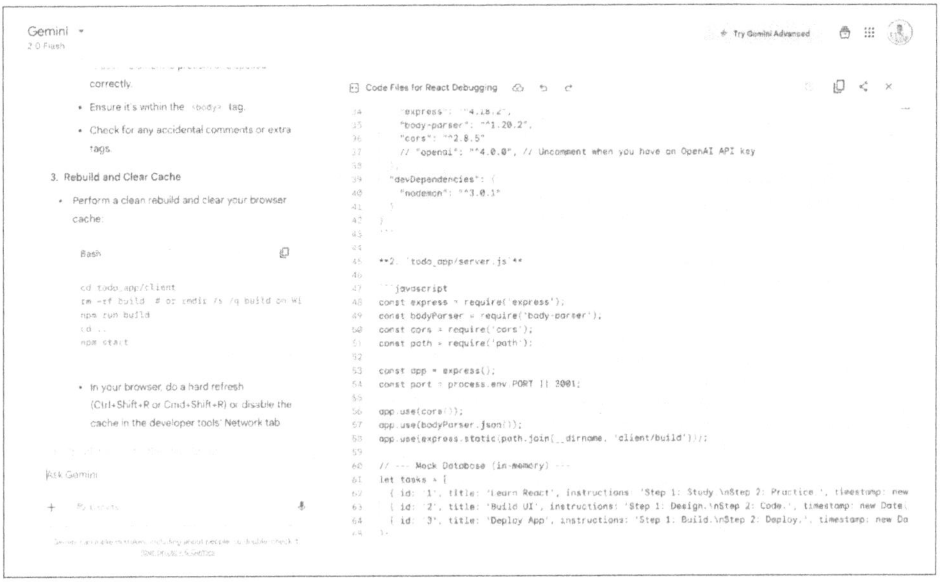

Figure 1-10. Gemini UI during the test

For all these reasons, Gemini's performance in this second test was very disappointing.

When I reviewed Gemini's code, I realized that it aimed for a stylish frontend that could have resulted in a crisp and modern UI, with TypeScript, Tailwind, Framer Motion, and Hero icons—except it didn't work. There was also an obvious error in the React code, where it was exporting the app component but not actually rendering it. This feels like an error that Gemini should have easily caught.

On the backend, the code seems to contain the desired functionality. However, it exposes the OpenAI API key in the actual code rather than using an environment variable. That's a serious security issue that would make this solution unacceptable for deployment or even testing.

Gemini provided the most disappointing experience of all the tools reviewed. First there was the clunky and error-prone experience of copy/pasting all code into the right files, then the errors in running both the frontend and backend, and then spinning its wheels to fix the React issues that prevented the UI from rendering properly. I ended up with no working solution even after spending significant time on this. With the caveat that Gemini produced a working solution for the first challenge and some relevant code for this second challenge, I rate it a 4/10.

GitHub Copilot

Copilot's solution ran nicely at first, since it uses minimal libraries and dependencies. It required a few debugging iterations when dealing with the structure of the OpenAI API request: first it was using the wrong endpoint, then the payload was structured wrong, then it had some parsing errors. But after a few minutes I had the working solution shown in Figures 1-11 and 1-12, with a very clunky frontend composed of vanilla HTML without much styling.

The button works, and when I add a new task, it does trigger the backend functionality. However, the frontend doesn't hide the modal pop-up when I'm done, nor does it have any "x" button to close it. It's visually underwhelming, and improving the UI would take multiple iterations.

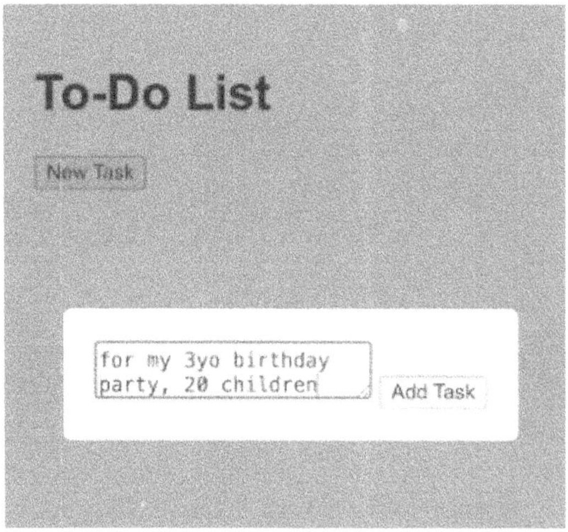

Figure 1-11. GitHub Copilot's solution—modal pop-up

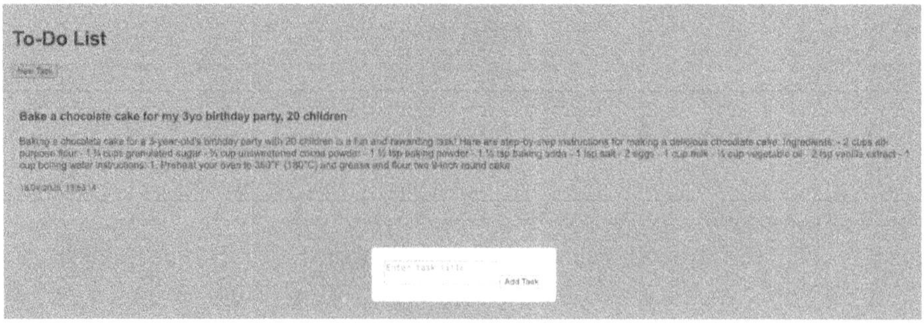

Figure 1-12. GitHub Copilot's solution—task added

From a code-review perspective, Copilot created a minimalist proof-of-concept, with plain HTML, CSS, and vanilla JavaScript on the frontend; a tiny Express server on the backend; and hardly any dependencies. The upside is total simplicity: anyone could read this code in minutes, and deployments are lightweight.

The trade-off is that every best-practice box stays unchecked: the OpenAI key is hardcoded. There's no database, no validation, no responsive design, and no framework ergonomics for future growth. It would be a great solution for a hackathon, but risky for anything user-facing without a major refactor.

I think there's merit in this approach, given that I didn't prompt Copilot with any specifics about the code quality or robustness I wanted. As a CTO, I appreciate starting simply, and Copilot did produce the simplest app of all tools reviewed for this challenge. I rate it 8/10 in this comparison test.

Cursor

Cursor separated its code into frontend and backend folders, and it was very easy to run each of them in Cursor with simple NPM start commands. The backend flow worked nicely. Both the database and the integration with the OpenAI API worked well, too, but the frontend was clunky. The baseline UI is weird, with the title on the very top and the "New task" button on the very bottom, as seen in Figure 1-13.

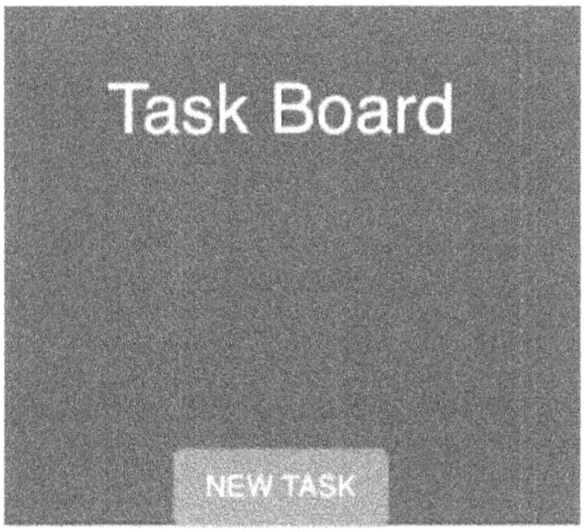

Figure 1-13. Cursor's solution UI

Once I click the "New task" button, a pop-up appears. It has decent styling but a one-line input field that cuts off any longer note descriptions, as seen in Figure 1-14.

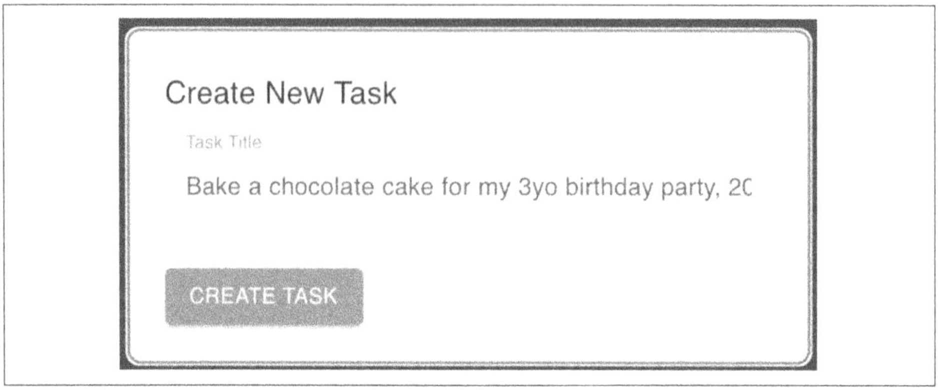

Figure 1-14. Cursor's solution UI pop-up

Once a task is created in the modal pop-up, the task cards are rendered below the button, at the very bottom of the screen (Figure 1-15).

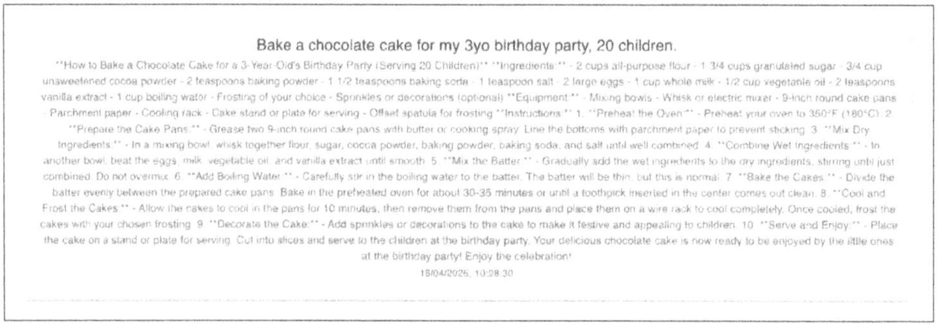

Figure 1-15. Pop-up in Cursor's solution

Cursor's solution actually implemented its functionality on the first try, making it very easy for me to run both frontend and backend. However, this solution didn't look like the Kanban board I asked for. It's a little better than Copilot's UI, but still a bit basic.

Looking into the code, I can tell that Cursor aimed for a sleek UI, using Material UI and react-beautiful-dnd. For some reason, though, that didn't translate into a pleasant UI. It also has the code well componentized and correctly uses environment variables, so the basics are solid. The backend is a bit barebones, with everything inside a single Express file with an in-memory array. There is no input validation and no error handling.

In a nutshell, Cursor's developer experience was unbeatable: it produced working code, and both the frontend and backend ran on the first try. The code works and fulfills the functionality, even if the UI isn't great and there's plenty of room for improvement under the hood. I rate Cursor a 9/10.

Windsurf

I found it challenging to get Windsurf's solution to work. It initially proposed an overly complex solution with unnecessary dependencies.

First, the frontend didn't run at all. Windsurf went down a "vibe debugging" rabbit hole with broken dependencies from Chakra UI, a frontend library that it decided to use. Eventually, I had to prompt it to not use that library at all so we could move on. Once the library was removed, the frontend finally ran (Figure 1-16).

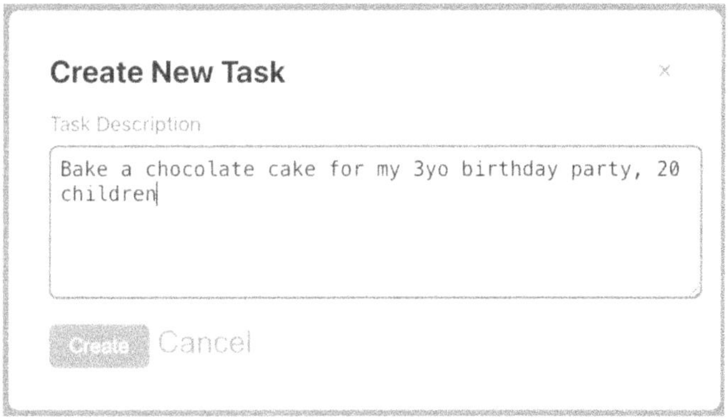

Figure 1-16. Windsurf solution UI

Then I had a similar challenge on the backend, this time with MongoDB dependencies. For some reason, Windsurf kept going down rabbit holes with such a simple task, and I ultimately had to prompt it to simplify the backend and use in-memory storage.

It finally ran and placed the task I created in the To Do column, in a proper Kanban UI (Figure 1-17).

Task Board　　　　　　　　　　　　　　　　　　New Task

To Do　　　　　　　　　　In Progress　　　　Done

Bake a chocolate cake for my 3yo
birthday party, 20 children

Steps for "Bake a chocolate cake for my 3yo
birthday party, 20 children". 1. Plan the task 2.
Execute the task 3. Review and verify
completion

18/04/2025, 13:23:16

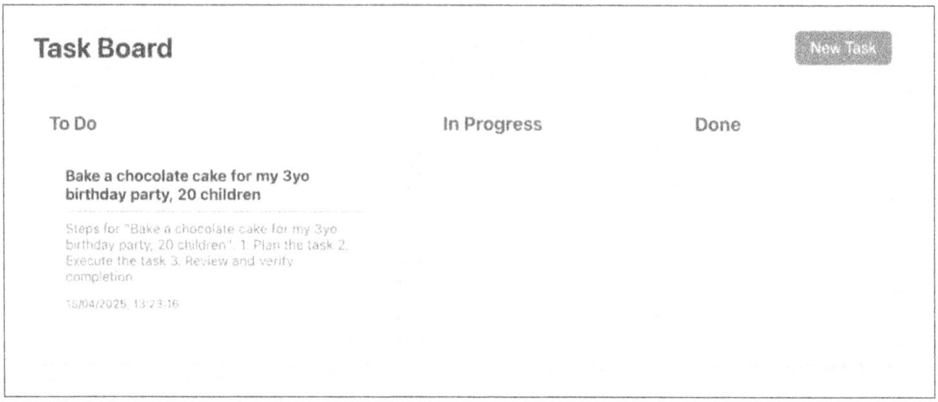

Figure 1-17. Windsurf Kanban board

However, it required me to drag the task to the In Progress column in order to trigger the OpenAI API request—but then crashed when I did so (Figure 1-18).

Task Board　　　　　　　　　　　　　　　　　　New Task

To Do　　　　　　In Progress　　　　Done

　　　　　　　　　　　　　　　　　Bake a chocolate cake for my 3yo
　　　　　　　　　　　　　　　　　birthday party, 20 children

　　　　　　　　　　　　　　　　　Steps for "Bake a chocolate cake for my 3yo
　　　　　　　　　　　　　　　　　birthday party, 20 children". 1. Plan the task 2.
　　　　　　　　　　　　　　　　　Execute the task 3. Review and verify
　　　　　　　　　　　　　　　　　completion

　　　　　　　　　　　　　　　　　19/04/2025, 13:30:55

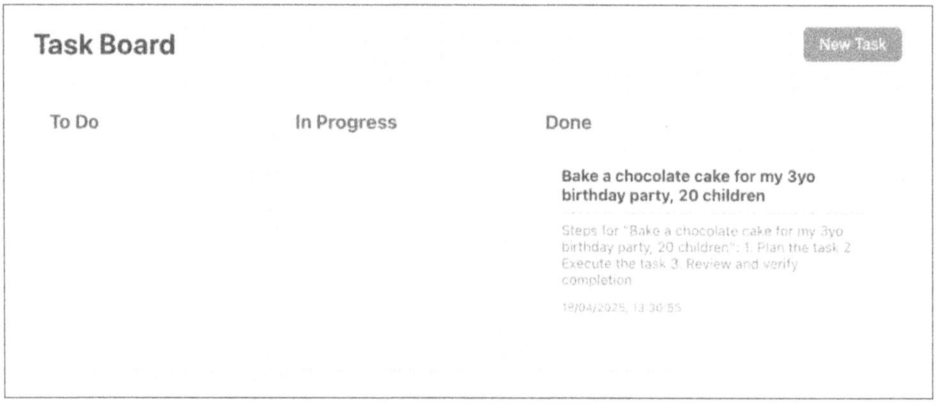

Figure 1-18. Windsurf solution

Again, I gave Windsurf more time to debug the issue, and finally, the app ran without errors. However, I found that it ran a bit "too fast," and the result was underwhelming. As it turned out, Windsurf had accidentally removed the code for the OpenAI API integration, one of the key features of the app (Figure 1-19).

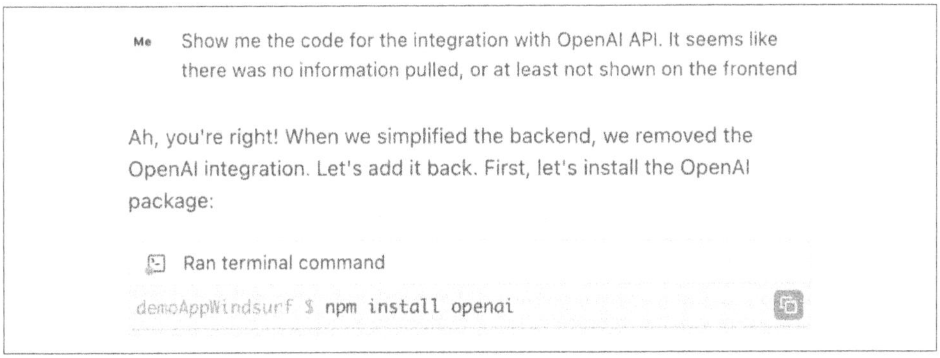

Figure 1-19. Windsurf accidentally removed the OpenAI integration

Finally, after a significant amount of time spent in these back-and-forth iterations, I finally had a working Windsurf solution that has an elegant Kanban UI and fulfills the backend functionality (Figure 1-20).

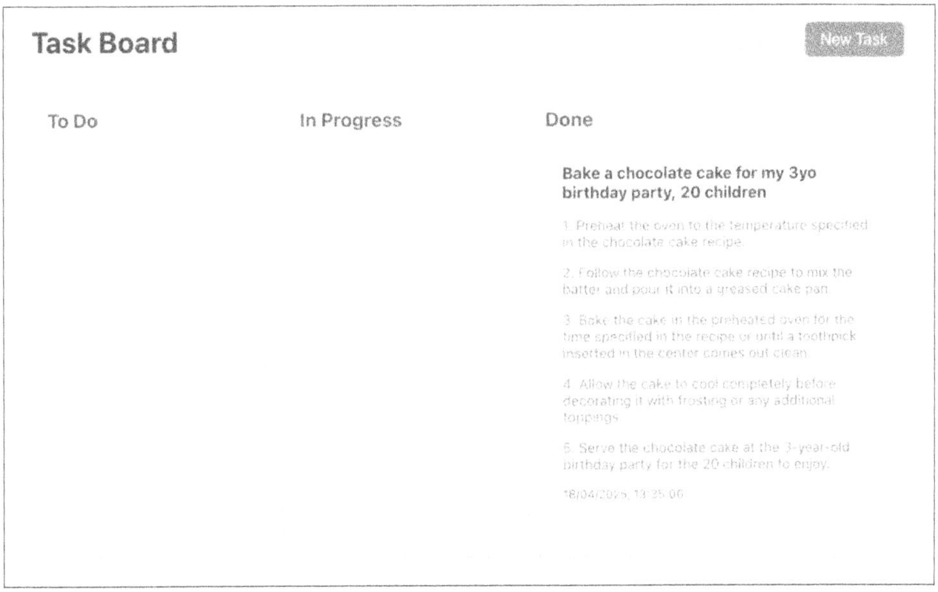

Figure 1-20. Finished Windsurf solution

In terms of code, Windsurf's solution is the most feature-complete: it uses React with drag-and-drop, modal creation, real-time refresh, and clean separation between routes, controllers, and components. Environment variables are respected, error handling is a bit more thoughtful, and the code style is consistent and easy to follow.

Interestingly, Windsurf took the most maximalist approach of this test. It tried to use fancy libraries that led it down rabbit holes it couldn't get out of on its own. I had to prompt it out of those three times, by instructing Windsurf to not use the dependencies that were creating trouble (first the Chakra UI library, then MongoDB, then the drag-and-drop). Its agentic approach makes Windsurf the most capable and seemingly independent tool I tested, even compared with Cursor and Copilot. However, that independence led it down dead ends a few times, and it takes an experienced developer to instruct it out of those dead ends.

Windsurf was also the tool that took me the longest to get to a working solution, over one hour. But it created the sleekest UI, and the code quality was quite good. I rate it a 9/10.

Table 1-1 compares my ratings for how well each of these tools performed in my testing.

Table 1-1. Code-generation tools overview

Tool	UX	Test performance
ChatGPT	Browser	8/10
Google Gemini	Browser	4/10
GitHub Copilot	IDE	8/10
Cursor	IDE	9/10
Windsurf	IDE	9/10

Conclusion

I've used the first test, the 2D-array code challenge, dozens of times in interviews over the years. It's incredible that all of the five tools reviewed in this test can produce the same outcomes as top-performing software engineers in only 10 seconds.

Clearly, these tools vastly outperform humans for these types of tasks: that is, tasks with clear requirements and input/output guidelines, where the code produced fits in a single file and for which there's plenty of relevant training data. All these interview-type challenges fit such a description, and more broadly, any of these LLM tools could likely solve any such algorithmic puzzle easily within seconds.

When I gave them challenges that included producing more extensive code repositories, some tools began facing difficulties, even for a simple Kanban UI with notes and backend automation. Using browser-based tools, such as ChatGPT and Google Gemini, makes it very burdensome to copy/paste the code into the right files. It's a lot of work, and it's very error-prone. It's an inferior experience compared to IDE-based tools that have both the code and the console terminal within their context window. As the developer, I don't need to copy/paste anything; it's all about reviewing and accepting or rejecting the suggestions. IDE-based tools make it feel like an efficient code review cycle, where I ask for changes, it codes them on the spot, and I review, accept, and test within seconds.

It's also clear that multiple state-of-the-art models from different providers are already capable of producing good software code. All of the IDE-based tools I tested (Cursor, Windsurf, and GitHub Copilot) allow developers to select a model from a drop-down list. Browser-based tools offer a more closed environment, with ChatGPT using only OpenAI's models and Gemini using only Google's models.

This means that the competition in this market is increasingly about the actual developer experience. Browser-based tools are out of this race, in my opinion. It's just too burdensome to share context with them, and then even more burdensome to copy/paste the code back to the repo. The winning solutions in this space will be based in the IDE, not the browser.

Even within IDE-based tools, there are different approaches. GitHub Copilot still has the original vibe of bringing a ChatGPT-like chat into the IDE, with access to the code and the ability to make changes. On the other hand, Windsurf takes it to a higher level of abstraction, with an agentic approach that creates folders and files, makes changes, and gives me a simple button to review the changes and "accept all," just like in a code review. Cursor is somewhere in the middle, with a better chat UX than Copilot, and provides users with the option to use its agentic mode (which I didn't use for this test).

From a software engineer's perspective, it's clear that our future work will be less about writing actual code and more about prompting these tools and reviewing the code they generate. This sounds much easier than it actually is, though. These tools create significant potential for driving entire codebases into a buggy and unmaintainable state, just like my scenario with Windsurf. Imagine a production-level codebase with hundreds of files, and Windsurf using its agentic mode to add random libraries and remove key parts of the backend functionality. I can see the potential for these tools to do a lot of harm if operated on a "vibe coding" basis, with developers mindlessly accepting suggestions without properly reviewing and testing the code.

As a software engineer, you should absolutely use these tools: they can help you ship product features faster and, in many cases, with a higher quality standard. However, you should *always* review AI-generated code before pushing it to production or opening a pull request. Make the code yours, regardless of how much of it was generated by an AI tool. There's decent potential for these tools to wreck your working code, so you should run the code they generate against a test suite that covers a wide range of cases, from the happy path to edge cases and error states. Getting all tests green is a solid confirmation that the code fulfills your requirements. And finally, be sure to revisit your company's guidelines for any AI tools you use for professional purposes.

CHAPTER 2

User Interface and User Experience Design

The world of software applications depends on beautiful *user interfaces (UI)* and intuitive *user experiences (UX)*. UI design is about how a product looks and how users interact with it visually. It focuses on layout, colors, buttons, typography, and everything that shapes the visual experience of a software product. UX design, on the other hand, is about how a product feels to the user and if it is intuitive and efficient to use. UX is about usability, navigation flow, and making sure the overall experience is smooth and user-friendly. Both work hand in hand to create great software products.

Producing those interfaces and experiences has been the job of UI/UX designers for the last few decades. They usually pair with software engineers to implement the functionality and the backend workflows that bring those designs to life as an integrated experience for users around the world. Transforming UI/UX designs into functional frontend code is a labor-intensive process, though. Traditionally, designers and engineers work closely to ensure that the visual aesthetics of a design are accurately translated into a responsive, interactive user interface. This process often involves multiple iterations, meticulous attention to detail, and a deep understanding of both design principles and coding standards.

Since the emergence of text-to-image generative AI models in 2022 and 2023, UI/UX design has witnessed an enormous transformation. As I write this in 2025, recent AI tools can now generate UI designs from ideas described in natural language *and* generate functional frontend code from UI designs. These tools are revolutionizing the design-to-code workflow by automating significant portions of the process. This has immense potential to reduce the time and effort required to bring designs to life and make design professionals much more efficient. AI tools can significantly reduce the gap between concept and implementation.

For example, the first iteration of wireframing and sketching designs for a new application can take more than a week to complete—sometimes more than a month, depending on the complexity of the project. The new AI design generators can cut wireframing time to less than a day and make each feedback loop faster as well. These tools' ability to transform designs into functional frontend code means one person or team can go from describing an idea in natural language to generating functional frontend code within minutes (or hours, counting iterations), as opposed to weeks or months.

This chapter will examine some of the leading tools in both the domains of UI design and UX design, aiming to cover the wide range of activities in between.

Types of AI Tools for Design and Frontend Development

Throughout this chapter, I'll focus on two types of AI tools: those that transform ideas into designs and those that transform designs into code.

Tools that transform ideas into designs
: This sounds like a UI/UX designer's job, but think about it: if creating designs becomes easier, faster, and more accessible to people without professional design skills, the average frontend developer will probably be able to create designs *and* code, as opposed to the current scope of work, which entails only writing code. That translates to massive empowerment for software engineers, especially those working on the frontend, who'll be able to create basic designs independently.

Tools that transform designs into code
: This segment complements the tools covered in Chapter 1, which generate code from a natural-language prompt. The tools here generate code from image-based mockups or Figma design files. (If you aren't familiar with it, Figma is for UI/UX designers what Visual Studio Code is for software developers.)

Most available UI/UX design generator tools are fully browser- and cloud-based. They are simple to use without complex software installation and are easily accessible with a browser and a URL. Some tools, like QoQo.ai (*https://qoqo.ai*), come as plug-ins for design platforms like Figma.

Most of the products this chapter covers have been launched very recently and are in the early stages of product development. They'll undergo continuous development, rolling out new features and improved functionality in the months and years ahead. As I write this, such design tools are a year or two behind software development tools like GitHub Copilot (*https://oreil.ly/6tmUG*) in terms of maturity.

I expect that in the UI/UX space we'll also see more browser-based tools, more add-ons or plug-ins to popular design platforms, and more integration into collaboration tools used between designers and frontend development teams. (The analogous tool to Git might still be Figma for many teams, but for others it might be plug-ins to popular collaboration tools like Jira or Notion—we'll see.)

Pros and Cons of Using AI Tools for UI/UX

Like any tools, the tools in this chapter present advantages and disadvantages. Some of the advantages include:

Efficiency and speed
: AI tools can process design files and components and generate corresponding code in a fraction of the time it would take a human developer. This rapid turnaround can accelerate project timelines and reduce costs.

Consistency
: By automating the conversion process, AI tools help maintain consistent implementation of design elements across a project.

Accessibility
: Individuals without technical or design expertise can pick up these tools and create functional interfaces, a shift that helps to democratize UI/UX design.

Prototyping and iteration
: AI-generated code allows for faster prototyping. Designers and engineers can quickly test and iterate on their ideas to bring new products to market much faster than ever before.

The drawbacks of the tools discussed in this chapter include:

Code quality
: Code produced by AI tools does not always meet the standards of human-generated code. It can be less efficient and harder to read and maintain, so—as I've emphasized throughout this book—developers must look through and revise generated code thoroughly before releasing it into production.[1]

Device compatibility
: AI-generated code may not be fully optimized for all browsers, operating systems, and screen sizes. This can lead to issues with responsiveness and cross-device compatibility that require additional effort to troubleshoot and fix.

Customization and flexibility
: While AI tools can handle standard design patterns well, they may struggle with more complex, custom design elements. This greatly limits creativity and the ability to tailor the design to specific needs. For this reason, human creativity is still needed.

1 This is yet another occurrence of the trade-off between saving time writing code and spending more time debugging, fixing, and improving code. It's not much different, conceptually, from the trade-offs of the HTML code generated by Dreamweaver in the early 2000s, or the more recent advent of low-code tools that generate templated code, which is often hard to customize and adapt to one's specific needs.

Lack of originality and uniqueness

AI tools often produce designs that resemble existing ones. These tools are trained on current designs and prevailing trends, which can lead to a lack of originality and distinctiveness, with some designs appearing generic or repetitive and failing to stand out. Although AI tools can offer a useful starting point or inspiration, they're far from matching the creative capabilities of a talented human designer.

Striking the right balance between leveraging AI for automation and relying on human talent for quality and creativity is key to successfully integrating these tools into the design workflow.

Use Cases for UI/UX AI Tools

UI/UX design-assistant tools aid different parts of the design process. They can be categorized as follows:

- Design ideation assistants
- User research and analysis tools
- Color palette and style generators
- Layout and component generators
- Accessibility checkers
- Personalization engines
- Voice-user interface (VUI) designers
- Gesture and motion design tools
- Wireframing and prototyping tools
- Design-to-code converters

This chapter focuses on the last two items, which lie at the intersection of UI and frontend code and are thus of most interest to software engineers. Other tools that target specific parts of the UX and product research workflows are usually more specific to designers and other roles that collaborate more loosely with software developers, like product managers, product analysts, and UX researchers.

Thus, I evaluate the tools in this chapter using the following use cases:

Rapid prototyping
: AI tools can quickly generate wireframes and prototypes based on initial inputs and design descriptions. This is a major chunk of the design process, where designers spend hours in back-and-forth iterations. With these tools, creating prototypes is much faster and designers can iterate multiple design options quickly. This flexibility can also make sophisticated flows such as A/B testing much more accessible.

Designing from templates
: AI tools can be trained on design principles like components, colors, and styles, to ensure consistency across different parts of a product by generating designs that adhere to established design systems, branding, and guidelines. This results in a cohesive user experience with uniform design elements and styles throughout the application. While this "factory" approach doesn't foster creativity, it does bring significant value for use cases where all you need is to create new screens that look like the existing ones but fulfill new functionality. (In all honesty, for better or worse, most software development consists of this "factory" approach, as proven by the growing popularity of low-code and no-code tools.)

Accessibility assessments
: AI tools can automatically check and improve the accessibility of UI designs for people with disabilities, ensuring compliance with standards like the Web Content Accessibility Guidelines (WCAG) and inclusive design practices—much as the tools covered in Chapter 3 do for software code. Such features can identify accessibility issues and suggest fixes, reducing the manual effort required.

User research and personalization
: AI UI/UX design tools can analyze user data about behavior, needs, and preferences to tailor their output to specific user groups or individuals, improving engagement, retention, and satisfaction. By leveraging data-driven insights, these tools ensure user-centered design. This can massively extend existing use cases. For example, if the goal is to create new landing pages for specific customer demographics, with these tools you could create full product variations according to specific parameters. Without them, each product variation would require a heavy software development cycle.

Content generation
: AI tools assist in generating content for UI elements, such as placeholder text, images, and icons. This quickly populates designs with realistic content, making prototypes more lifelike for testing and ensuring consistency with the design's style and tone. This frees designers to focus on the more creative aspects of the process.

Evaluation Process

My process in this chapter was as follows: I submitted a brief design prompt to each of the selected UI design tools, ran the same challenge on each tool, and compared their output. I also evaluated their ability to convert the designs they generate into frontend HTML CSS, Next.js, and React code. I reviewed 20+ tools available in the market. As expected, they followed a long-tail distribution: a few worked as advertised, while others delivered poor output or had different issues that prevented me from running the test. Many tools in the AI space were developed by startups whose products are in very early stages of development.

After trying the tools, I selected the best four in each category that provided actual value for the use cases tested. I then rated each tool on a scale from 1 to 10, with 1 being the worst (a solution that errors out and doesn't run at all), 10 being flawless, and 5 being a design that didn't exactly fit the requirements. I look closely at the top product in each category, detailing its pros and cons, then provide more concise information on the runner-up.

It's also important to note that all tests described in this chapter were run in spring 2025. Given the fast pace of evolution of each of these tools and their underlying models, it's likely that you could get a different result at a later time for the same prompt.

UI Tools

I asked each of the AI tools covered in this chapter to generate screen designs for a mobile food delivery application. Here is the detailed prompt I provided:

```
Create a user-friendly food delivery app that allows customers to browse
local restaurants, view menus, place orders, and track delivery status
in real-time. The app should include these screens: Login, Restaurant
and Menu Browsing, Order Placement, and Tracking.

Style: App should be modern and minimalist, focusing on ease of use and
visual appeal. The design should incorporate a clean layout. Add in
mouth-watering food images.
```

Let's see how the tools did.

Uizard

Uizard (*https://uizard.io*) has a marketing slogan that I believe sets the standard for most other players in this space: "Forget no-code, here comes no-design." The analogy between code automation and design automation makes a lot of sense. Just as no-code has promised the same functionality in a fraction of the time and budget, no-design could have an equal impact on the design process.

The Uizard product started as a machine learning research project called pix2code in 2017 in Copenhagen, Denmark. According to Uizard's marketing collateral (*https://oreil.ly/Yeeio*), "It allows developers to visualize product ideas quickly and easily with AI. This helps to fast-track the workflow of designers and software developers. Its mission is to democratize design and empower non-designers everywhere to build digital, interactive products."

At the prompt screen (Figure 2-1), I asked Uizard to generate screens for a food delivery app using the prompt from the preceding section.

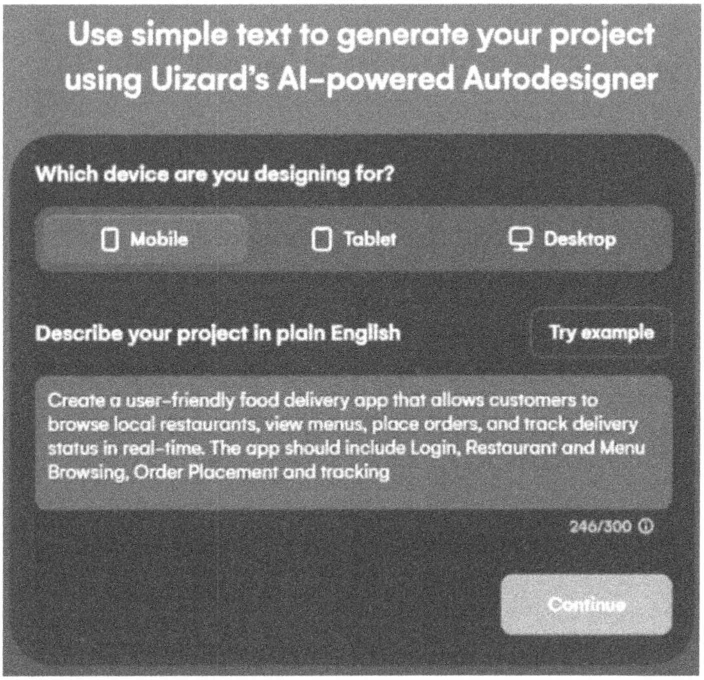

Figure 2-1. The Uizard Autodesigner prompt screen

Figure 2-2 shows the designs it generated.

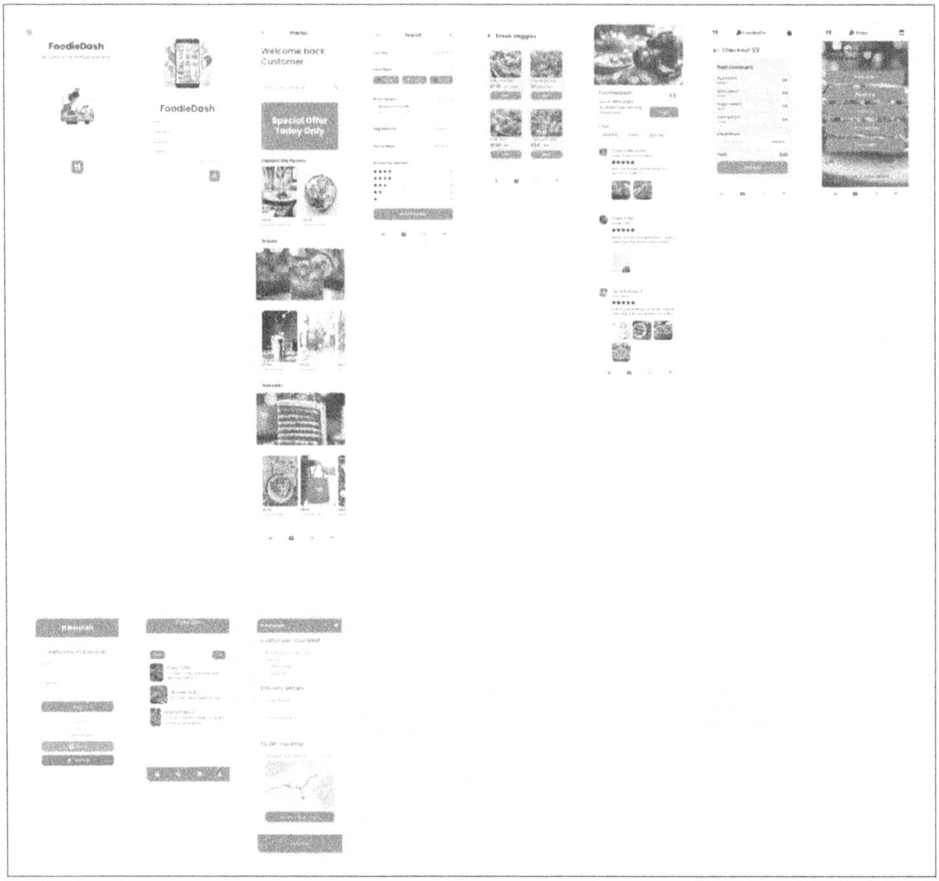

Figure 2-2. Screens generated by Uizard (11 in total)

You can see all of the screens it generated, along with the interactions, as previews on Uizard's site (*https://oreil.ly/GfXvV*).

One of Uizard's unique features is that it creates an interactive demo of the designs, with actual interactions and transitions between screens. This makes it a go-to website for transforming an idea into a demonstrable concept, even before writing any code. On the other hand, Uizard doesn't generate code to the level of other tools in this space, such as Bolt.new or Lovable, which generate working code alongside the designs and make it easy to commit the code to GitHub and even to deploy the working app right away.

I rate Uizard an 8 out of 10. Its design component is very competent, but it falls short in generating working code.

Bolt.new

Bolt.new (*http://bolt.new*) is a browser-based, AI-powered development tool launched in October 2024 by StackBlitz. It enables users, including those without technical skills, to create frontend web and mobile applications using natural-language prompts. By integrating technologies like WebContainers, Supabase, and Netlify, Bolt.new allows for seamless code generation, authentication, and deployment directly from the browser. This approach simplifies the development process, making it accessible to a broader audience.

The platform has experienced rapid growth, achieving $20 million in annual recurring revenue (ARR) within two months of launch and reaching $40 million ARR by February 2025.[2] With over three million registered users and one million monthly active users, Bolt.new has become one of the fastest-growing AI tools in history. Its success is attributed to its user-friendly interface, efficient development workflow, and the ability to swiftly transform ideas into functional applications.

I gave the same prompt to Bolt.new, and it generated the app designs seen in Figure 2-3.

The screens generated are very solid, with the pages, navigation, and hierarchy I'd expect in such an application. It generated realistic mock text and images for each screen, making them look good. There's an obvious glitch in the footer, with both missing icon images and creeping navigation, but other than that the designs are very good.

What's best about Bolt.new is that it can help *beyond* generating designs from a natural-language prompt: it also generates the underlying code. In this case, it generated frontend code in TypeScript.

2 Akshay from Startup Spells. March 22, 2025. "Bolt.new: The 2nd Fastest-Growing Product in History (Behind ChatGPT)" (*https://oreil.ly/nnAaP*). *Startup Spells*.

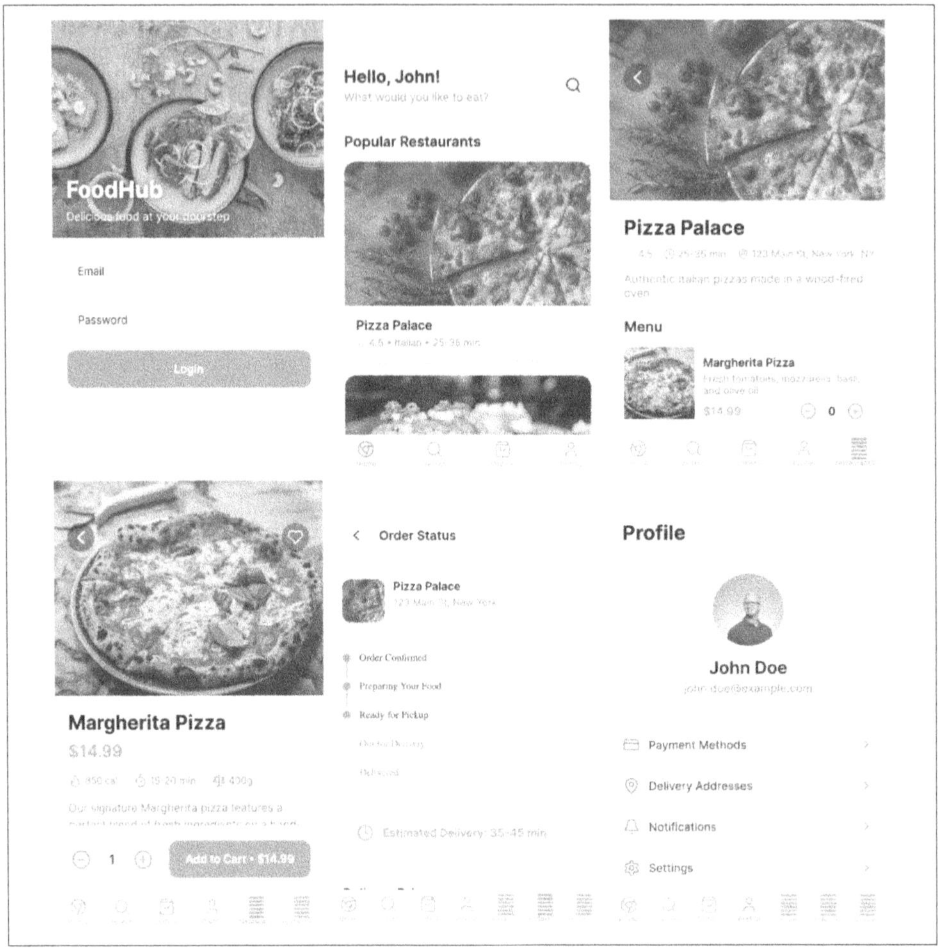

Figure 2-3. Screens generated by Bolt.new

As seen in Figure 2-4, the Bolt.new workspace consists of:

- A prompt area on the left, where I can ask for new screens, changes, fixes, etc.
- A code editor, where I can see the actual code being generated and make live changes
- A console, where I can see errors, logs, and anything else resulting from the code execution
- A preview area where I can see all screens, such as the screenshots in Figure 2-3
- Options to export and deploy my application

Figure 2-4. The Bolt.new workspace

Bolt.new is a one-stop-shop that aims to fully replace not just designers, but also IDEs and cloud providers—since, when I published my app, it was hosted on Bolt.new's servers. Given the comprehensive feature set, I rate Bolt.new a 10 out of 10.

Lovable

Lovable (*https://lovable.dev*) is a browser-based AI development platform launched in November 2024 by the Swedish startup of the same name. It empowers users, both technical and nontechnical, to build full stack web apps using natural-language prompts. By combining tools like Supabase for backend services and GitHub for version control, Lovable automates everything from database setup to deployment. The result is a dramatically simplified development experience, allowing anyone with an idea to launch functional software directly from their browser.

In just three months, Lovable reached $17 million in ARR and attracted over 30,000 paying subscribers. With more than 50,000 new projects started each day, it's one of the fastest-growing AI dev tools to date.[3] Much of its momentum comes from its intuitive interface and ability to abstract away the traditional complexity of software development, making the field—especially frontend interfaces—more accessible than ever.

3 Stephane at Lovable. February 25, 2025. "Announcing $15m Added Funding to Build the Last Piece of Software" (*https://oreil.ly/UuLvM*). *Lovable* (blog).

I gave the same prompt for the food delivery app, and Lovable generated the app designs shown in Figure 2-5.

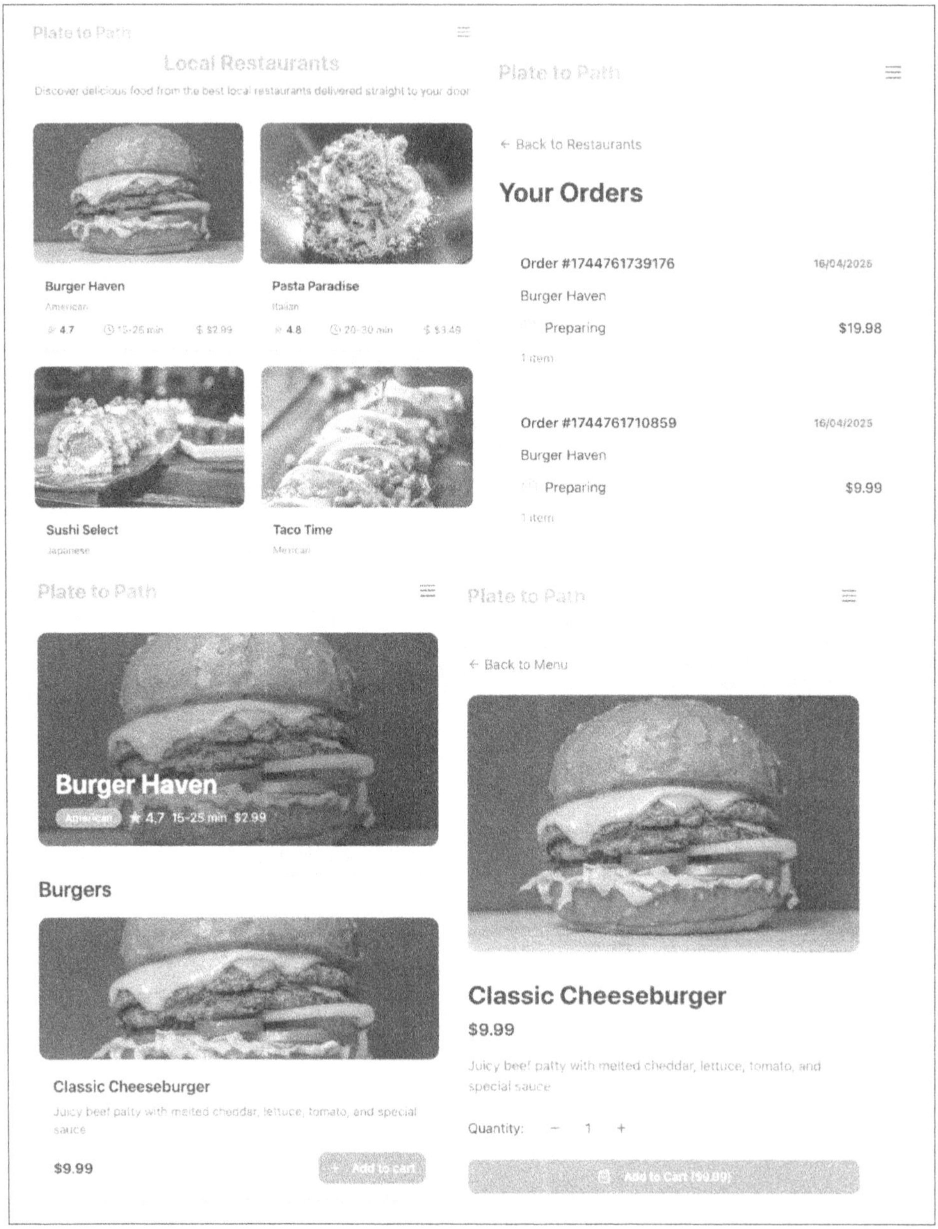

Figure 2-5. Screens generated by Lovable

Very similar to Bolt.new, Lovable has a chatbot UI on the left side of the screen, allowing the user to prompt with natural language for new screens, changes, fixes, etc. It also has a toggle on the top to switch between preview and "Dev mode." The preview mode shows the generated designs, as seen in Figure 2-5, while Dev mode shows the code produced. On the top, there are buttons that allow users to easily sync the code with GitHub or deploy the app.

I also rate Lovable a 10 out of 10. I think it's the leading player in this space alongside Bolt.new. Both fulfill the use case of getting professional designs and working code from a natural-language prompt.

UX Tools

In this short section, I cover tools for the UX part of the UI/UX design workflow: user research, product workflows, and usability.

Here is the prompt I used for evaluating UX tools:

```
Create a user persona for an 18-25-year-old university student trying
to order food online from a restaurant using our application.

Description: 18-25, Female, Male, University undergraduate from
Los Angeles, California, single, and no children. Looking for a
user-friendly platform to order food very fast, track orders, and
make payments
```

QoQo.ai

QoQo.ai (*http://qoqo.ai*) (pronounced "cocoa") is an AI-for-UX-design Figma plug-in that helps in the early stages of design. Designers can use it to generate UX personas, journey maps, site maps, and UX copywriting. UI/UX designers, product managers, and product researchers, who usually do these tasks, will save time with this tool; it can also make these tasks more accessible to software engineers, helping them better engage with users.

I provided QoQo with the preceding prompt, and within seconds the AI generated a detailed user persona (shown in Figure 2-6).

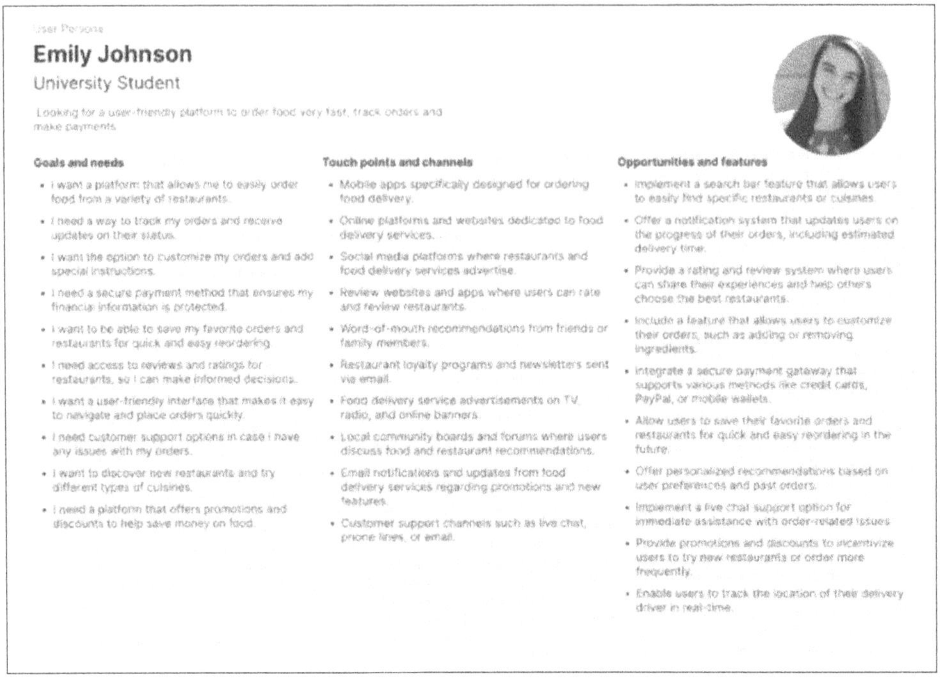

Figure 2-6. QoQo user persona

I rate QoQo an 8 out of 10. It gets the job done, and there is really no learning curve involved. It does feel like a GPT wrapper, in the sense that it's generating text and placing it into predefined brackets, which can provide tremendous value if you are starting to design the UI/UX of a software product.

Research Studio

Research Studio (*https://researchstudio.ai*) is an AI-powered application designed to automate the customer and user research analysis process. This tool is particularly useful for researchers and designers who need to transform user interviews into actionable insights, analyze satisfaction, and generate branded reports swiftly. Traditionally, UX researchers spend hours combing through vast amounts of data to extract insights. Research Studio streamlines this process, making it faster and more efficient.

Research Studio's platform allows you to choose between three open source LLMs: Claude AI, Mistral, or OpenAI's GPT-4o. You upload your user interviews and it extracts insights into a report. It can also use the information it has garnered from the interviews and data to write a report. Several report types are available as outputs, including user flows, feature maps, and question analysis.

To evaluate this tool, I used Claude AI (separately) to generate some raw input. I asked it to generate 50 survey responses from users of our dummy food-delivery app, using the following prompt:

```
Generate 50 survey responses from users of a food delivery app, reflecting their
thoughts after using the app for some time. The responses should highlight both
positive and negative views, including any problems they faced and suggestions
for features that could improve the app's efficiency and user experience.
```

These responses included both positive and negative feedback, as well as suggestions for improvements. Here are a few examples from Claude's output (*https://oreil.ly/2zbPd*):

```
1. "The app is fast and easy to use. Love the variety of restaurants!"

2. "Delivery times are often longer than estimated. Please improve accuracy."

3. "I wish there was an option to schedule orders in advance."

4. "The customer service is excellent, always helpful when I have issues."
```

I passed the responses into Research Studio to extract insights (Figure 2-7) and asked it to write a comprehensive report based on its built-in report types (Figure 2-8).

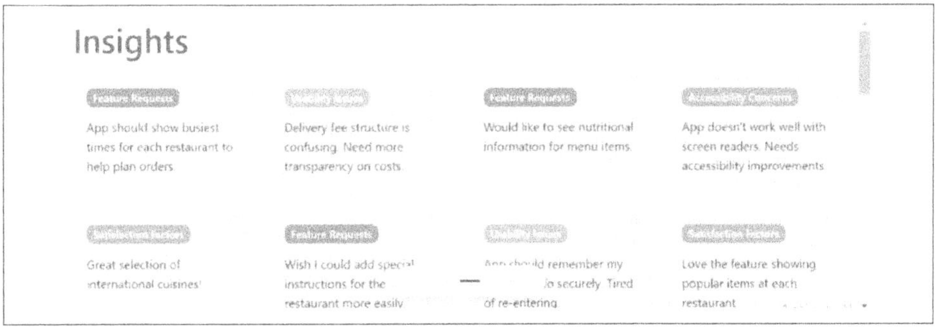

Figure 2-7. Research Studio transformed raw user reviews into a map of "insights"

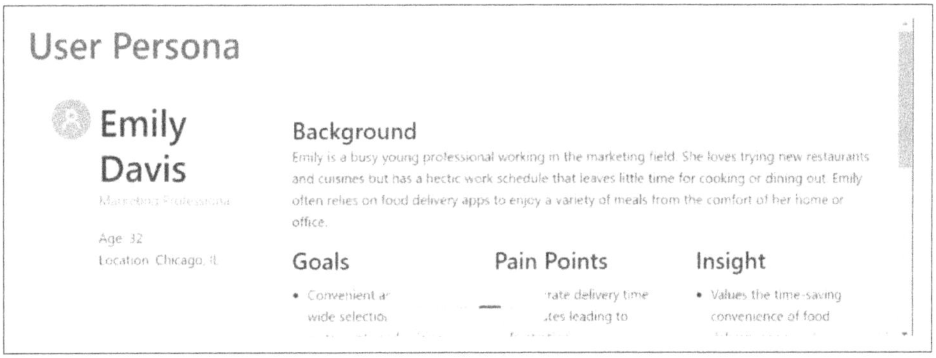

Figure 2-8. An insight map generated by Research Studio from survey responses

These tools make software engineers capable of producing working designs, and given the staggering pace of their development, I can foresee that many teams will no longer need specialized designers to produce lots of screens. Of course, specialized interactions, branded UI elements, or complex user-experience nuances will still be best served by specialized human UI/UX designers. But I can imagine that most standard app flows, such as registration flows, listings, and profile pages, will be well served by these AI tools.

Never before have software engineers been so empowered to collect feedback from the users of their products, structure that feedback into actionable insights, generate improved designs, transform them into code, and push a new iteration to production. Product iteration cycles will shorten significantly thanks to these tools. Professionals who master them will have much more market demand than those who stick to only writing code. As I write these lines in early 2025, I'm seeing big growth in the Product Engineer job title in recent months, which caters exactly to this opportunity I'm describing: software engineers who can understand the client's needs, convert them into product feature descriptions, and ship the code that fulfils those descriptions.

CHAPTER 3

Bug Detection and Code Review

Imagine paying the highest salaries in a company to software engineers to develop a product that will be responsible for the company's revenue, only to lose that revenue due to costly bugs in production. This is any business owner's worst nightmare, and sadly it happens every day. Software has automated whole industries, replacing lengthy manual processes and creating new ways to do previously impossible things. However, automation can't be effective when bugs detract from the underlying products' key functionalities.

To mitigate this fundamental concern, several job titles have been created over the years to guarantee proper quality assurance (QA), such as QA engineer, QA analyst, and test engineer. Processes, too, have been developed to detect bugs before they get deployed to production. Those processes boil down to two main categories:

Code reviews
: This process is done during development, and it consists of team members reviewing each other's code before it is deemed ready to go live. Some teams mandate a minimum number of team members who must review and approve a pull request (PR) before it can be merged.

Quality assurance
: This process is done after development as the last "gatekeeper" before code gets pushed to production. It consists of manual or automated tests done in an environment that closely matches production. These tests aim to mimic users' behavior to catch any bug that could have escaped a code review.

When either process finds any bugs, performance issues, security vulnerabilities, or other malfunctions, the code can be *regressed;* that is, it goes back to the software engineer who developed it, along with a comment containing the specific deficiencies that must be corrected.

These processes are critical to any software development team, yet they are often very lengthy and nondeterministic, introducing bottlenecks while not fully delivering on the vision of preventing bugs from showing up in production. As such, as AI tools have come into existence, the industry has seen a big focus on automating code reviews and making the process of detecting bugs much faster and more deterministic. Thousands of software engineering teams are already using AI-based automated code-review tools.

Types of AI Code-Review Tools

The AI tools reviewed for this chapter fall into three main categories, with slightly different usage in software development. Some of the tools reviewed offer more than one type of functionality.

IDE-based tools
: IDE-based tools integrate directly into the software development environment that engineers use to write code, such as Visual Studio Code, IntelliJ IDEA, or Eclipse. These tools provide real-time feedback as developers write code: highlighting errors, suggesting improvements, and providing documentation links directly in the IDE. Of the three types of tools described here, this is the only type that provides feedback when the code is saved locally. This immediate feedback loop helps developers identify and fix issues on the spot, improving code quality and reducing the need for extensive reviews later.

Git-based tools
: Git-based tools integrate with version-control systems, such as GitHub, GitLab, or Bitbucket, and operate within the Git workflow. Unlike IDE-based tools, Git-based tools can't be triggered by local saves of a file, only by actions in the Git workflow. You can set them up to review code automatically whenever you push changes to a repository or create or merge a PR. These tools check the code against predefined rules and guidelines and can enforce coding standards across all branches of the codebase. They typically provide feedback in the form of comments in PRs or reports in a continuous integration pipeline, helping ensure code quality before merging changes into the main branch.

Browser-based tools
: These tools are accessible through web browsers and typically integrate with online version-control platforms like GitHub, GitLab, and Bitbucket. Like Git-based tools, they can only be triggered by changes in the Git workflow, not local changes. You can use these browser-based tools to get automatic reviews of your PRs or code merges online. When you submit a PR, the tool reviews the code for errors, style violations, and security vulnerabilities, then provides feedback on that PR via the web interface in the browser. I find this the least convenient of the three types of tools presented here, since it requires you to use another platform besides the IDE and version-control tools you are already familiar with.

It's also important to differentiate between linters, static analysis tools, and AI-powered code-analysis tools:

Linters
: These are the simplest of these tools, focusing primarily on enforcing coding standards and styles. They scan code to identify syntax errors, stylistic inconsistencies, and basic programming errors. Linters like ESLint for JavaScript (*https://eslint.org*) and Pylint for Python (*https://oreil.ly/-wu0d*) are integrated into development environments, providing real-time feedback to correct issues like indentation, bracket placement, and line length.

Static analysis tools
: These tools delve deeper, analyzing code without executing it in order to detect potential bugs, security vulnerabilities, and performance issues. Static analysis tools, such as SonarQube (*https://oreil.ly/wrZII*), understand control flow, data flow, and variable scopes, making them capable of identifying complex issues like memory leaks and concurrency problems. They are commonly integrated into CI/CD pipelines, helping to maintain code health across projects.

AI-powered code analysis
: These tools use machine learning to analyze coding patterns across many projects, identifying complex issues and suggesting improvements. AI analysis tools, like DeepCode and Codacy, provide context-aware suggestions and can predict the impact of code changes, offering optimization tips learned from vast datasets.

Due to the scope of this book, I'll only cover this last type of tool, AI-powered code analysis.

Use Cases

The millions of software engineers who are already using AI tools for automated code reviews and bug detection find that they bring obvious benefits across a range of daily use cases. These include:

Educating software engineers
: Automated code-review tools provide software engineers, especially more junior ones, with a 24/7 pair programmer that points out bugs, offers suggestions, and above all gives context and reasoning for its suggestions. This is a great tool to hone your skills. Feedback loops are much more frequent with an automated tool than with normal code reviews by team members, increasing exposure to learning opportunities about the language, framework, or algorithm in question. This is extra beneficial for junior developers and for engineers switching to new tech stacks or working with a framework for the first time, since lack of experience makes mistakes more common. In code reviews, errors can be regressed with a message that helps the developer understand the mistake and avoid it next time.

Increasing software development velocity
: Automating code review reduces the number of PR regressions. It also tremendously reduces the amount of time between the code being written and the review identifying issues to be fixed. Automatic code reviews at every change can point out vulnerabilities and improvements so that developers can fix them immediately. This eliminates the cycle of pushing faulty code only for other team members to find and regress it—a cycle of multiple regression loops that cost individual developers time and delay shipping features to production.

Reducing tech debt
: Many times, code reviews overlook security vulnerabilities and performance issues because they don't usually impact functionality, which is objectively the biggest focus of any code review. Even when they are detected, they aren't often treated as cause for regression. Instead, they often go into a "nice to have" note, effectively adding the vulnerability or issue to the pile of tech debt. That pile usually accumulates for a long time, until it becomes unsustainable and requires extensive refactoring of the codebase.

Adding depth to code reviews
: Most of the code-review tools mentioned in this chapter focus on security vulnerabilities and often point out occurrences of OWASP Top 10 vulnerabilities in code, along with suggestions for resolving them. Team code reviews rarely reach this level of depth; such vulnerabilities are often only detected much later (if ever), during professional security audits or penetration-testing reports. Using these tools allows teams to detect security vulnerabilities much earlier.

Keeping the Human Review

A common criticism of automated code-review tools is that they discourage (human) team members from performing code reviews in a timely manner. To be fair, code reviews were a dreaded activity in many teams long before AI tools came into existence. Software engineers frequently forget to review their peers' pull requests or leave a positive review message of "lgtm" (short for "looks good to me") just to unblock a feature deployment.

AI tools add tremendous immediacy to the code-review process. This reassures software engineers that their code has a high quality standard, but it also leaves them feeling less urgency to review their peers' code, believing the AI tool has already done that job for them.

This is a very fair criticism, in my opinion. *AI code reviews don't replace human code reviews*, especially those performed by senior engineers who know both a feature's technology and the business and use cases for it. This is the angle that is manifestly missing in AI code reviews. The AI tool misses the *context* behind the code being reviewed and the intent behind certain code segments. This can lead it to make irrelevant suggestions or fail to identify context-specific issues that might be obvious to a human reviewer. This is a key reason why you should *never skip human code reviews*, even if you're also using automated code reviews.

It's also worth noting that the language used to market these automated code-review tools is quite different from that used for the code-generation tools reviewed in the previous chapter. Few of the tools discussed in this chapter mention AI in their marketing copy much (or at all), despite the fact that the products do use AI algorithms (e.g., Codacy).

There are two reasons for this. Several of these tools existed in the market for years before the recent popularity of AI. However, many position themselves as a backstop to issues found in AI-generated code. Sonar (*https://oreil.ly/ODAHw*), for example, promises to minimize risk, ensure code quality, and derive more value from code created by both AI and humans. As the website copy states: "To maximize the advantages of generative AI in coding, developer teams need robust DevOps processes, reporting, and metrics that focus on code quality, security, and reliability."

Evaluation Process

I evaluated more than 20 automated code-review tools in order to shortlist the ones I highlight in this chapter. Every tool covered here meets the following criteria:

- It is a professional project with a competent team behind it.
- The code it generates has a high quality threshold.
- It offers some level of functionality for free or on a trial basis.
- It has a high level of adoption at the time of writing (mid-2025).

In order to select and compare AI tools for this chapter, I created a simple JavaScript program and introduced four issues into the code. You can review the full code in the book's GitHub repository (*https://github.com/sergiopereira-io/oreilly_book*), inside the folder named "Chapter 3." Example 3-1 provides the most relevant snippet, with each of the four issues commented for clarity. I ran the exact same code through each of the tools reviewed in this chapter, which discusses the results each tool provided.

Example 3-1. Code snippet for the tests of code-review tools

```
app.post('/submit', (req, res) => {
   const requestData = req.body;

   // 1. SQL Injection vulnerability
   const sqlQuery = `SELECT * FROM users
                     WHERE username = '${requestData.username}'`;
```

```
    db.all(sqlQuery, [], (err, rows) => {
        if (err) {
            console.error('Error executing SQL query:', err.message);
            res.status(500).send('Error in database operation');
        } else {
            console.log('Query result:', rows);
            res.send('Data processed with SQL query results: '
            + JSON.stringify(rows));
        }
    });

    // 2. Cross-Site Scripting (XSS) vulnerability
    const responseHtml = `
        <html>
            <body>
                <h1>User Profile</h1>
                <div>${requestData.userInput}</div> <!-- User input is
directly rendered into HTML -->
            </body>
        </html>
    `;
    console.log('Generated HTML for user:', responseHtml);

    // 3. Potential memory leak in event listeners
    const listeners = [];
    for (let i = 0; i < 100; i++) {
        listeners.push(() => console.log('Event listener', i));
    }
    console.log('Number of listeners created:', listeners.length);

    // 4. Inefficient loop
    let sum = 0;
    for (let i = 0; i < 100000; i++) {
        sum += i;
    }
    console.log('Sum of 0 to 99999:', sum);
});
```

Before we dive in, here is a brief explanation of each of the errors I introduced and why it would be important to catch them in a code review:

SQL injection vulnerability

This vulnerability arises from incorporating user input directly into a SQL query without any form of validation or sanitization. In the provided code, the variable `requestData.username` is directly concatenated into the SQL query string. This approach lets attackers craft user inputs that manipulate the SQL query to perform unauthorized actions, like accessing, modifying, or deleting data. For instance, an attacker could provide a username input like `' OR '1'='1`, which could alter the query logic to return all users in the system, thereby breaching data privacy.

Cross-site scripting
: *Cross-site scripting* (XSS) occurs when an application includes untrusted data, typically from user inputs, within the content of its web pages without proper validation or escaping. In the script, `requestData.userInput` is directly included in an HTML response structure sent back to the client. If this user input includes malicious JavaScript code, the browser could execute that unauthorized script, leading to session hijacking, personal data theft, or malicious redirection.

Memory leak
: *Memory leaks* in web applications can occur when memory that is no longer needed is not released back to the system. In the example, a large number of event listeners are created within a loop but are never removed. Each listener retains a closure scope that may consume more memory. Over time, especially in long-running applications like servers, these listeners accumulate, occupying an increasing amount of memory. This can potentially exhaust available resources and lead to performance degradation or crashes.

Inefficient loop
: The loop in the example code inefficiently performs a large number of iterations to compute the sum of all integers from 0 to 99,999. Each iteration involves performing arithmetic operations and updating a local variable. Although these actions are relatively simple, they are unnecessarily repeated many times. This not only consumes CPU cycles, but it could also block the event loop in a Node.js environment, leading to delays in processing other incoming requests or operations.

Now let's dive into the top-performing AI code-review tools I tried.

Codacy

Codacy (*https://www.codacy.com*) is a startup based in Portugal that launched an automated code-review tool in 2012. The product has evolved significantly over the years and is now a market-leading solution that leverages AI to "help developers identify and fix issues within their code, improving code quality and reducing technical debt, with support for more than 40 programming languages and seamless integrations with GitHub, Bitbucket, and GitLab," as per the copy on its website.

Codacy's AI tool analyzes code for potential errors, style violations, security vulnerabilities, and performance issues, and it provides software engineers with suggestions for improvement. The tool is designed to learn from past reviews, adapting to the specific standards and practices of each development team.

By automating the code-review process, Codacy helps developers focus more on building features rather than fixing issues, ultimately speeding up the development cycle and enhancing code maintainability.

Practical example

I created an account with Codacy using my GitHub account and ran the tool on the code shown earlier in this chapter (which you can review in full in the book's GitHub repository (*https://github.com/sergiopereira-io/oreilly_book*)).

Codacy correctly identified issue number 1, the SQL Injection vulnerability, and labeled its severity as "Critical," the highest level in its ranking, as seen in Figure 3-1.

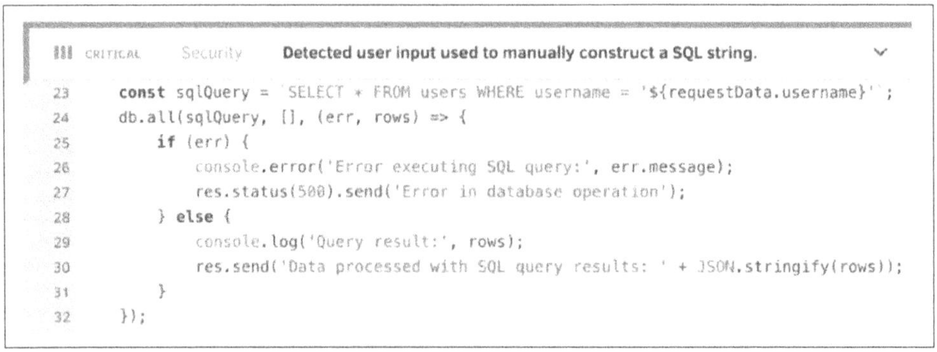

CRITICAL
Security
Detected user input used to manually construct a SQL string.
const sqlQuery = `SELECT * FROM users WHERE username = '${requestData.username}'`;
db.all(sqlQuery, [], (err, rows) => {
if (err) {
console.error('Error executing SQL query:', err.message);
res.status(500).send('Error in database operation');
} else {
console.log('Query result:', rows);
res.send('Data processed with SQL query results: ' + JSON.stringify(rows));
}
});

Figure 3-1. Codacy identified the SQL injection vulnerability

Codacy provides an expandable section with an explanation of what the error is, why it's dangerous, and how to solve it (Figure 3-2).

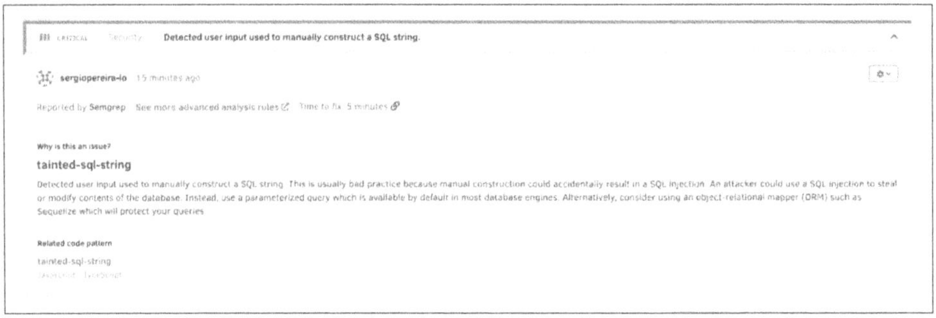

Figure 3-2. Codacy explained the SQL injection vulnerability

I rate Research Studio a 7 out of 10. While it feels like a simple LLM wrapper, it does a good job with the workflow, and it does deliver value for anyone who wants to crunch massive amounts of data into structured product insights to use in their next software-development iteration.

Tool Comparison

Galileo AI emerged from my evaluation as the best text-to-UI tool among the 20+ tools I evaluated, including the four featured in this chapter. Its ability to take an image and remake it into a beautiful design also makes it stand out. As I've noted, this space is still in its very early days, so I can only imagine how far these tools will evolve in the coming years.

The UX tools I evaluated are less complex in terms of underlying technology, but that's not a critique: they worked well enough for their use cases.

Table 2-1. AI UI/UX tools overview

Tool	Purpose	Test performance
Uizard	UI generation	7/10
Bolt.new	UI and code generation	10/10
Lovable	UI and code generation	10/10
QoQo.ai	UX automation	8/10
Research Studio	UX automation	7/10

Conclusion

I began writing this chapter with the wrong expectations. I didn't expect the tools in this space to be very useful in their current state, given their newness. I was wrong. I'm now very excited about this space and the evolution in software development processes we'll see in the coming months and years.

Generating frontend code from designs, with the increasingly dominant use case of generating both design and working code from a prompt (as seen in Bolt.new and Lovable), is certainly the angle that best speaks to software engineers, especially those working on the frontend. It is a game-changer that will save software engineers around the world millions of hours.

The other use cases seem to cater less to software engineers, as they are designers' work. But think about it: our tools are becoming more powerful, and if it takes less time to do the same work, software engineers can manage a larger portion of design workflows. Indeed, our employers and team leads will likely ask us to do so more and more.

Codacy also correctly identified issue 2, the XSS vulnerability, and labeled it as "Medium" severity (Figures 3-3 and 3-4).

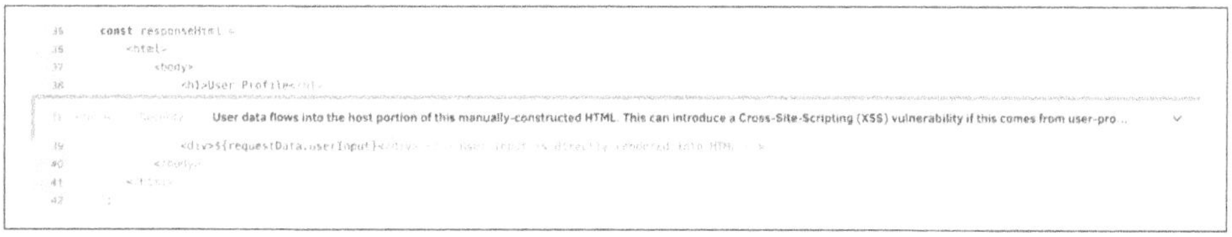

Figure 3-3. Codacy identified the XSS vulnerability

As seen in Figure 3-4, Codacy clearly explained this XSS vulnerability.

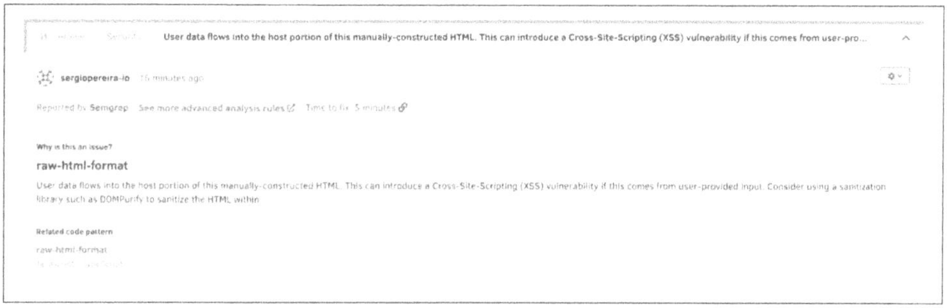

Figure 3-4. Codacy explained the XSS vulnerability

Codacy's analysis didn't identify issues 3 and 4, which are more related to performance than to security.

All of this feedback was provided on Codacy's website immediately after I connected my GitHub account and selected the repository I wanted to have analyzed. However, after I opened a PR on that same repository, Codacy performed a second level of analysis directly in the repository.

Most of the errors it identified reiterate those it found in the previous analysis, which I expected, since the code is the same. However, on GitHub, Codacy also offers a "commit suggestion" to fix each issue along with a brief explanation. This makes it very convenient for software engineers to simply accept the suggestion and merge the PR with one click (Figure 3-5).

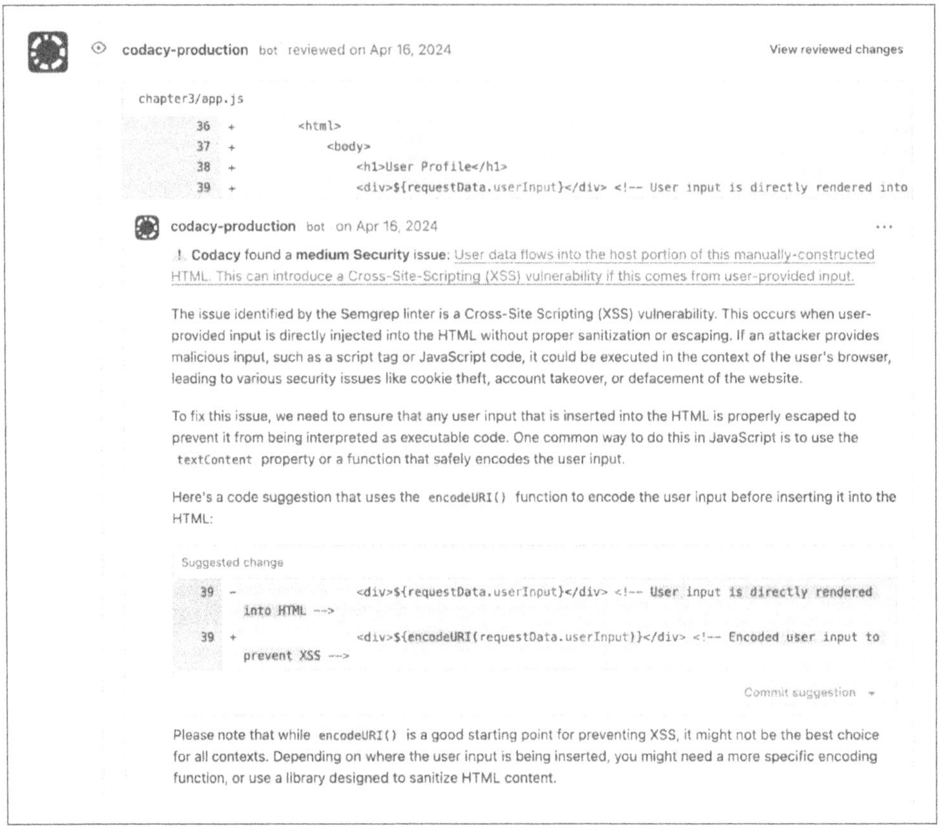

Figure 3-5. Codacy suggested a fix for the issue it found

For all these reasons, I rate Codacy's tool an 8/10. It found two of two security issues, but it didn't find either of the two performance issues. For the issues it did find, it offered very comprehensive explanations and proposed fixes that could be accepted in the actual repository with one click.

DeepCode (by Snyk)

DeepCode (*https://oreil.ly/VBZWA*) began as an independent startup based in Zurich, Switzerland, as a spinoff from ETH Zurich University.[1] It was acquired by the cybersecurity behemoth Snyk in September 2020.[2] Since then, the product was marketed

1 This book's author was part of the DeepCode team prior to the company's acquisition by Snyk, but has no contractual relationship, equity, or any other vested interest in DeepCode at the time of writing.

2 McKay, Peter. September 23, 2020. "Accelerating Our Developer-First Vision with DeepCode" (*https://oreil.ly/jdWJl*). *Snyk* (blog).

first as "DeepCode by Snyk" and more recently as "DeepCode AI," and has been integrated into Snyk's broader suite of products and services.

As Snyk described it (*https://oreil.ly/jdWJl*) in 2020, DeepCode includes "sophisticated interpretable machine learning semantic code analysis. The technology scans code 10–50x faster than alternatives, enabling real-time workflows within the development process, and dramatically reduces both false negatives and false positives using a custom machine learning platform that is able to quickly learn from huge volumes of code."

DeepCode uses machine learning algorithms to learn from millions of publicly available open source software-development repositories. This large dataset allows DeepCode to provide highly accurate suggestions and find potential issues that human reviewers might overlook.

DeepCode can be used on an IDE or directly in a Git repository. It points out security vulnerabilities on the spot, as alerts in the IDE tool tip or as comments to the pull request in the repository. As the company's website (*https://oreil.ly/VBZWA*) puts it:

> It combines symbolic and generative AI, multiple machine learning methods, and the expertise of top security researchers to offer accurate vulnerability detection and tech debt management. DeepCode AI is purpose-built for security, supporting 11 languages and over 25 million data flow cases to find and fix vulnerabilities efficiently. This AI technology enhances developer productivity by offering one-click security fixes and comprehensive app coverage while ensuring the trustworthiness of the AI through training data from millions of open-source projects. DeepCode AI stands out for its hybrid approach using multiple models and security-specific training sets to secure applications effectively.

Practical example

Just like I did for Codacy, I created an account with Snyk/DeepCode using my GitHub account and ran it on the code in Example 3-1 within the book's repository.

DeepCode correctly identified issue 1, the SQL injection vulnerability, and labeled it with "H" (High), the highest level in its ranking system. It even provides a score (Figure 3-6), though I could not find specific information about what this score means. This issue's score of 830 is the highest score received by my code.

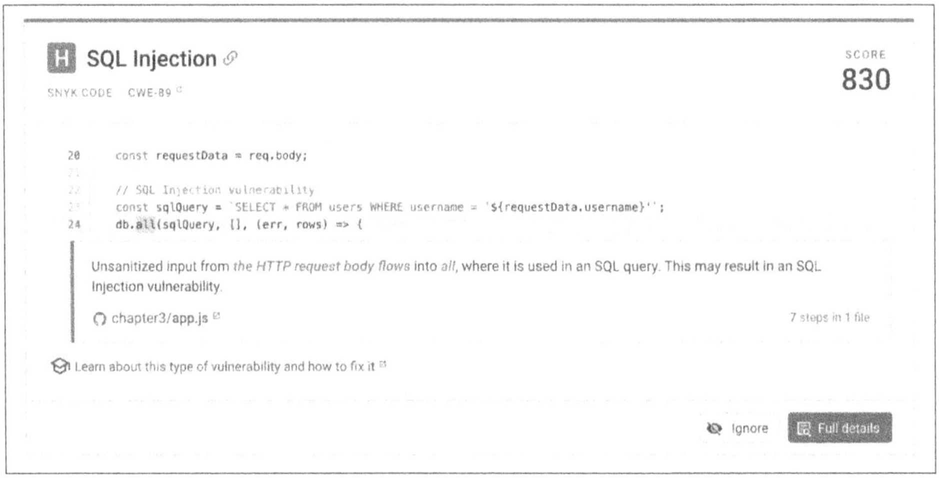

Figure 3-6. DeepCode identified the SQL injection vulnerability

Snyk/DeepCode provides two expandable sections for each error. One provides a deeper explanation of the issue, resembling a stack trace rendered in the browser UI (Figure 3-7).

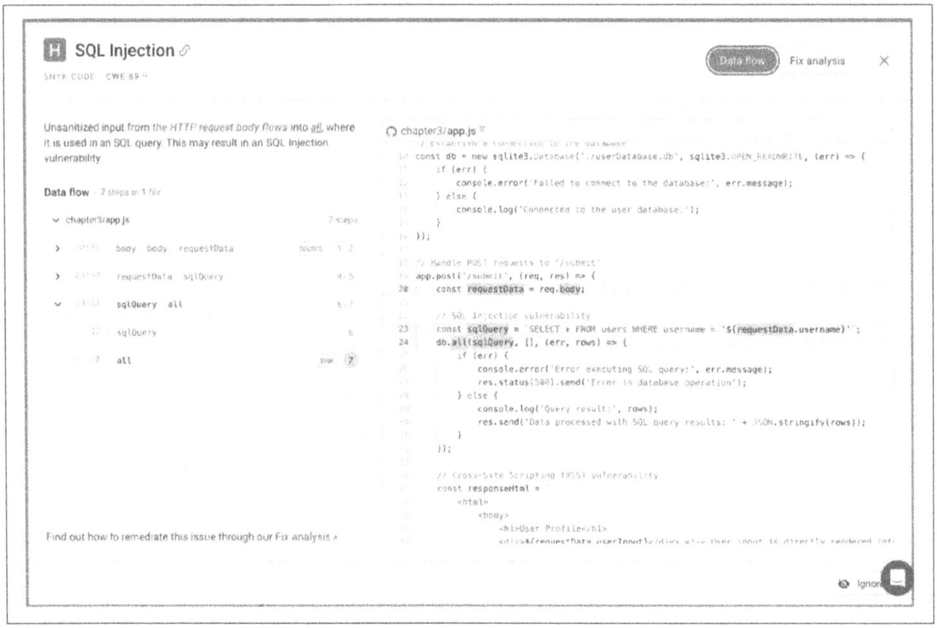

Figure 3-7. DeepCode explained the SQL injection vulnerability

The second expandable section suggests a fix for the issue (Figure 3-8) and gives pointers to avoid using concatenated SQL statements as strings stored directly from user-entered parameters. This is a best practice in defensive programming.

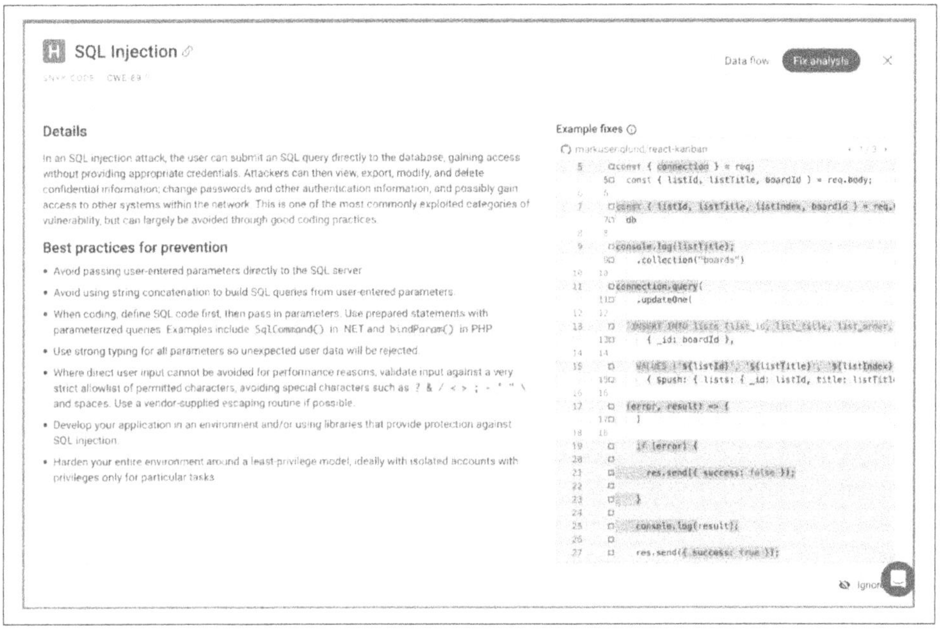

Figure 3-8. DeepCode suggested a fix for the SQL injection vulnerability

These suggestions are provided "as is" from an open source repository in the training dataset. This is very nice in terms of transparency, as a software engineer should always want to know where the code comes from. However, it adds some extra cognitive load in terms of actually solving the problem, since this is just a proposed solution to help the software developer fix the issue, not an actual proposed solution to be adopted with the click of a button.

Despite this deep level of detail for issue 1, DeepCode didn't find issues 2, 3, or 4. It did find some lower-severity issues in some libraries I used (inside `node_modules`), which were irrelevant to this book's exercise.

I rate DeepCode a 6/10. It found one of two security issues and didn't find either of the performance issues. For those issues it found, it provided very comprehensive explanations; however, the help it offers for each issue is lacking in comparison to that offered by Codacy and CodeRabbit. DeepCode provides information about the issue, but it doesn't offer proposed solutions that are easy to adopt with one click.

CodeRabbit

CodeRabbit (*https://coderabbit.ai*) is an automated code-review platform launched in September 2023, amid the generative AI buzz. It gained significant popularity very fast, especially on Twitter/X as some tech influencers did thorough reviews of the product and promoted it in their networks (here's one example (*https://oreil.ly/m9rjn*)). The official number of CodeRabbit users had not been publicly disclosed at the time of writing (mid-2025).

CodeRabbit leverages AI capabilities to enhance the quality, performance, and efficiency of code reviews. It delivers its code recommendations through comments in the repository.

Practical example

Like I did for the other tools, I created an account with CodeRabbit, allowed it access to my GitHub account, and selected the repository I wanted to give it access to. Unlike Codacy and DeepCode, CodeRabbit won't statically analyze code that's already in a repository. Instead, I needed to open a pull request; CodeRabbit then posted comments to that PR with its code-review items and suggestions. CodeRabbit promotes this as a much more interactive tool that aims to mimic a team member commenting on a PR seconds after it's opened on GitHub. However, my experience on CodeRabbit's website was greatly inferior to my experiences with the competitors analyzed here.

CodeRabbit correctly identified issue 1, the SQL Injection vulnerability (Figure 3-9). It doesn't provide any indication of severity level: all issues it reports look alike in that regard. It did a good job pointing out the faulty code snippet and offered a brief explanation about why it contains a vulnerability. I believe most software engineers will enjoy this simple UI, since it's exactly the type of interaction they get from human colleagues who review their PR.

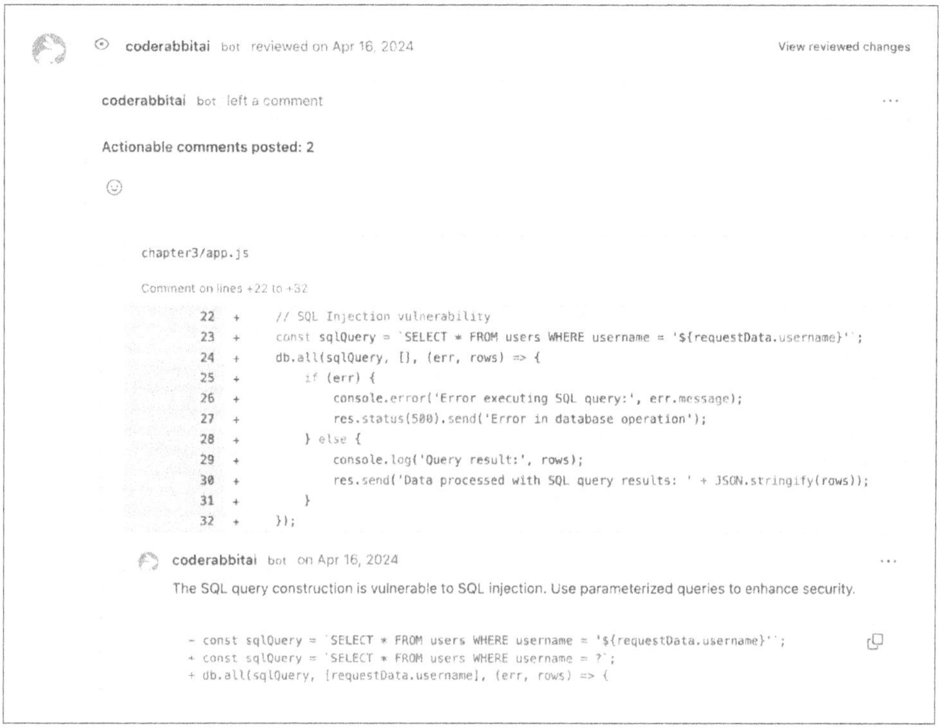

Figure 3-9. CodeRabbit identified the SQL injection vulnerability

Along with the explanation, CodeRabbit offers an expandable section called "Committable suggestion" that contains a suggested fix for the issue (Figure 3-10). While CodeRabbit displays a noticeable warning to review the offered solution thoroughly, committing it is only one convenient click away.

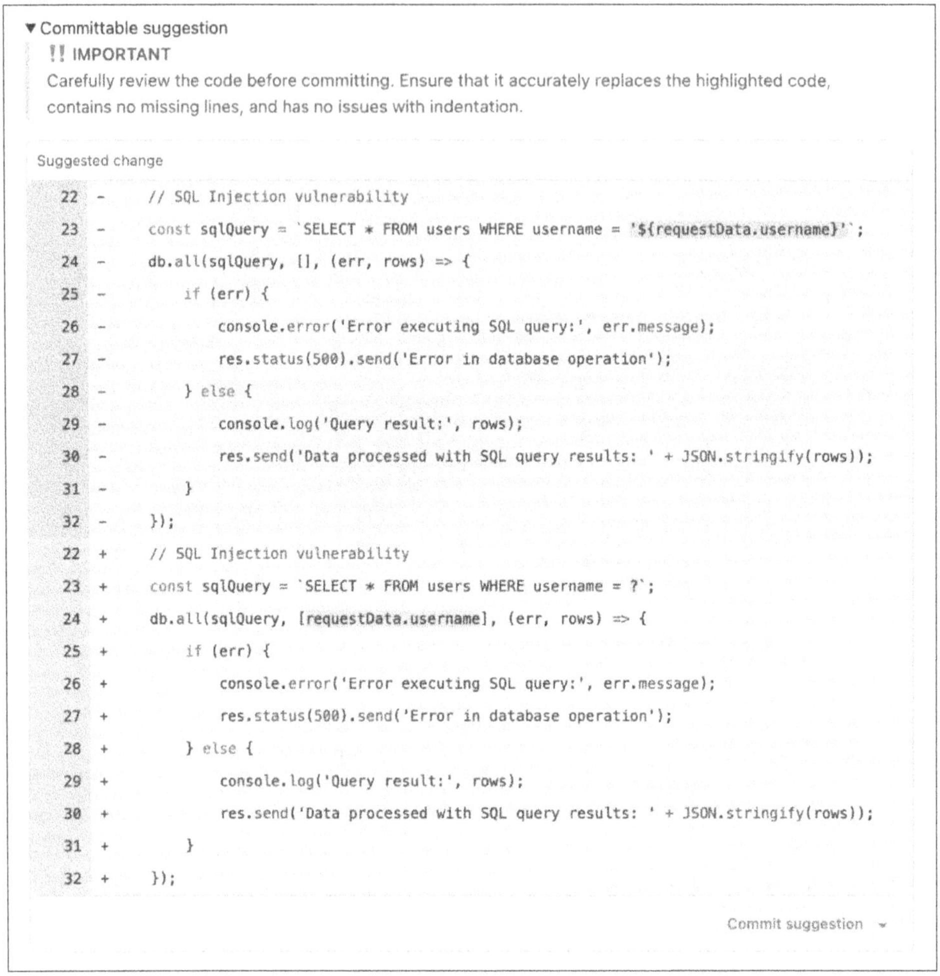
▼ Committable suggestion

‼ IMPORTANT

Carefully review the code before committing. Ensure that it accurately replaces the highlighted code, contains no missing lines, and has no issues with indentation.

Suggested change

```
-    // SQL Injection vulnerability
-    const sqlQuery = `SELECT * FROM users WHERE username = '${requestData.username}'`;
-    db.all(sqlQuery, [], (err, rows) => {
-        if (err) {
-            console.error('Error executing SQL query:', err.message);
-            res.status(500).send('Error in database operation');
-        } else {
-            console.log('Query result:', rows);
-            res.send('Data processed with SQL query results: ' + JSON.stringify(rows));
-        }
-    });
+    // SQL Injection vulnerability
+    const sqlQuery = `SELECT * FROM users WHERE username = ?`;
+    db.all(sqlQuery, [requestData.username], (err, rows) => {
+        if (err) {
+            console.error('Error executing SQL query:', err.message);
+            res.status(500).send('Error in database operation');
+        } else {
+            console.log('Query result:', rows);
+            res.send('Data processed with SQL query results: ' + JSON.stringify(rows));
+        }
+    });
```

Commit suggestion

Figure 3-10. CodeRabbit suggested a fix

CodeRabbit also detected issue 2, the XSS vulnerability (Figure 3-11), but just like the other tools analyzed, CodeRabbit didn't find performance issues 3 and 4.

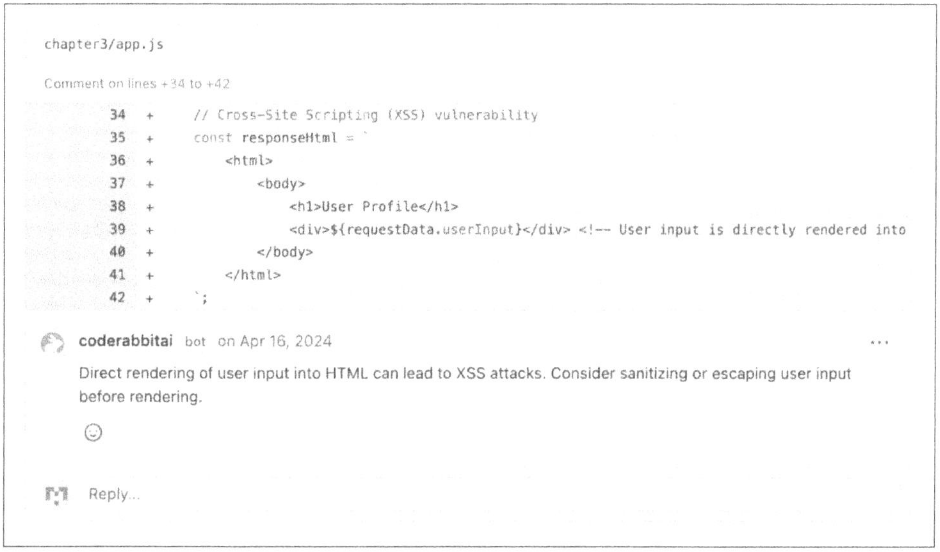

chapter3/app.js
Comment on lines +34 to +42
34 + // Cross-Site Scripting (XSS) vulnerability
35 + const responseHtml = `
36 + <html>
37 + <body>
38 + <h1>User Profile</h1>
39 + <div>${requestData.userInput}</div> <!-- User input is directly rendered into
40 + </body>
41 + </html>
42 + `;
coderabbitai bot on Apr 16, 2024
Direct rendering of user input into HTML can lead to XSS attacks. Consider sanitizing or escaping user input before rendering.
Reply...

Figure 3-11. CodeRabbit identified the XSS vulnerability

Thus, I rate CodeRabbit a 7/10. It found both security issues but neither of the performance issues. It also proposed a solution for one of the issues it found, but not the other one. However, its explanation for the issues was very superficial compared to the other two tools. Finally, it lacks a website interface that would let users research issues in more depth and provide some historical perspective of changes and improvements made on the codebase, which the other tools have.

Tool Comparison

All three of these AI code-review tools take different approaches to blocking my pull request from being merged, as shown in Figure 3-12:

- Codacy blocks the PR merge until I fix the issues it identified (which, to be fair, I can do using its suggested fixes).
- Snyk/DeepCode doesn't block the PR merge, despite the issues found.
- CodeRabbit only posts comments; it doesn't run actual checks, and thus it would never block a PR merge regardless of any issues it finds.

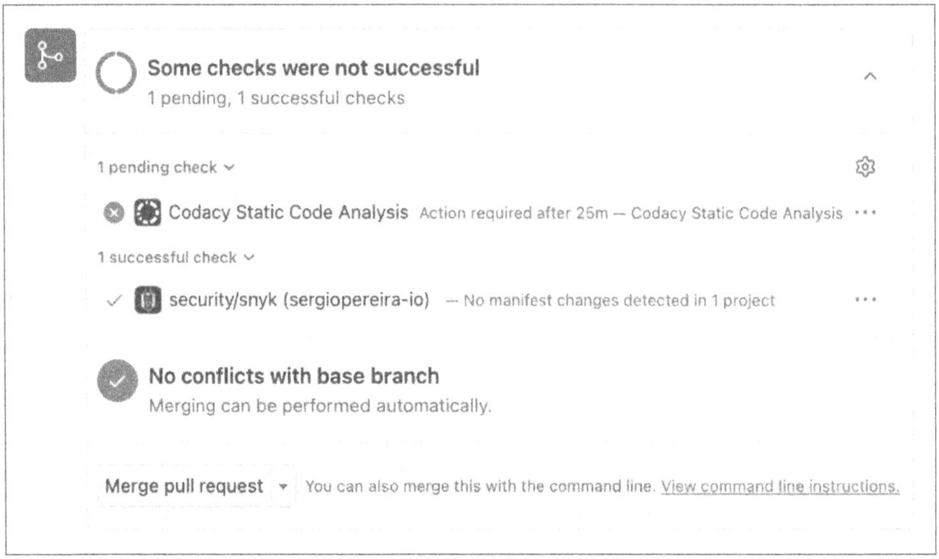

Figure 3-12. Codacy and Snyk/DeepCode show up in the checks section for the PR merge

If I were to select a single tool, Codacy would be my go-to tool. As Table 3-1 indicates, it had the highest score.

Table 3-1. AI code-review tools overview

Tool	UX	Test performance
Codacy	Browser + Repository	8/10
Snyk/DeepCode	Browser + Repository	6/10
CodeRabbit	Repository	7/10

Conclusion

Code reviews have been one of the biggest frustrations in my software development teams over the years. People are naturally more inclined to pick up new tasks assigned to them than to stop their own thread of work to review a colleague's PR. This default behavior has delayed features from being moved to QA and ultimately going live. It has also created situations where we fast-track some urgent features even with a less-than-ideal level of code review, resulting in bugs showing up in production. In general, the biggest casualty of these common code-review frustrations is team morale, with team members feeling like they're constantly switching context and losing focus.

I began using several forms of automated code review in my teams, like linters, static code analysis, and test coverage dashboards, long before the recent generative AI hype. Any team with robust engineering standards has probably done likewise.

However, after 15 years in the industry, I can tell that the recent wave of evolution adds more depth to these tools—especially the seamless way they integrate with your software development workflow, and the option to accept suggested fixes with one click. Having a very capable code reviewer who's available 24/7 to provide thoughtful feedback on issues in your code is a massive help to anyone. It's something I could only have dreamed of when I started out as a software engineer myself.

However, I believe that software engineers should leverage these tools as learning opportunities before anything else. They can and do make mistakes, as the tools themselves note in very visible warnings, and I can only underline that. *Always* have a human being review and test the suggested fixes. As with code-generation tools, I recommend a high level of diligence when reviewing any code or fixes suggested by these tools. Make it yours before you open a PR or merge to master.

CHAPTER 4

Automated Testing and Quality Assurance

Testing and quality assurance (QA) are usually the last gates that new software code must pass through before it gets deployed in production. Their ultimate goal is to find costly bugs or other standout issues that may have made it through code review (as covered in the previous chapter) to avoid putting them into production.

The QA process happens after code has been developed, reviewed, and accepted to merge into the codebase. There is occasional confusion between testing and QA as concepts, perhaps because the stakeholders traditionally involved are called either testing engineers or QA engineers at different companies. Whatever the title, though, they are usually in charge of the process covered in this chapter.

Typically, the QA process consists of conducting manual and/or automated tests in an environment that closely matches production and mimics user behavior, to catch any bugs that escaped the code-review process.

When such bugs are found during testing/QA, the feature is regressed back to development status. The original software engineer in charge of implementation must fix the issues before pushing the feature to review and QA again. These regression loops aim to guarantee that the code that ultimately gets deployed to production is indeed bug-free.

These processes are critical to any software development team. We can break them into two main categories: automated and manual.

Automated tests

Automated testing employs specialized software tools to execute pre-scripted tests on the application. This method is highly efficient for repetitive and regression tests, because it reduces the time needed to validate new code changes. Automation ensures consistency and precision, minimizes the risk of human error, and enables extensive test coverage. Automated tests can run around the clock, providing rapid feedback and allowing for continuous integration and continuous delivery (CI/CD) pipelines. Although initially setting up automated tests requires effort, as does maintaining them, the long-term benefits include faster release cycles, improved accuracy, and the ability to quickly detect and address defects.

Manual tests

In manual testing, human testers meticulously execute test cases without the assistance of automated tools. They simulate end-user behavior to identify defects, ensuring that the software behaves as expected in real-world scenarios. This approach allows for nuanced understanding and adaptability, often catching issues that automated scripts might miss, such as user-interface glitches and usability concerns. While manual testing can be time-consuming and labor-intensive, it remains essential for exploratory testing, where creativity and intuition are crucial in uncovering unexpected bugs and ensuring a seamless user experience.

QA is a meticulous, careful process by its nature, which often makes it a bottleneck that delays features going live. As such, there's a market for AI tools that propose to accelerate different parts of this process. This chapter will focus on two of those tools in particular.

AI is changing every aspect of automated testing. For example, until very recently, automating testing involved writing complex scripts. Now, however, many automated testing tools provide ways to create tests without writing a single line of code. With simple, plain English, you can create automated tests that check every component and functionality in your software application. Visual testing has also been simplified with AI-powered tools that automatically detect visual bugs, ensuring that your user interface looks and works as intended. These improvements make the testing process more effective and efficient, which allows testers to focus on improving the overall quality of the software.

Types of AI Testing Tools

In addition to the automated/manual divide, we can also classify AI tools for software testing and quality assurance as *functional* and *nonfunctional*, based on the specific areas they target within the testing lifecycle.

Functional AI testing tools
: As the name implies, *functional* testing tools verify that a software application performs all of its intended functions accurately. These tools focus on what the system does. Their goal is to test whether the application's internal components deliver the expected output. Functional testing tools handle unit tests, integration tests, visual tests, regression tests, and smoke tests, for example.

Nonfunctional AI testing tools
: *Nonfunctional* AI testing tools assess aspects of software that go beyond its functional behavior, such as its performance, compatibility, usability, security, and reliability. These tools focus on evaluating the software's *performance* rather than its behavior. They measure speed, response time, and resource utilization, to name a few.

Tools in both categories aim to identify potential performance issues and security vulnerabilities. They use deep learning models trained on customer usage data, internal company documents, or even industry regulatory norms or standards. These algorithms can learn to identify patterns that may indicate performance bottlenecks or security risks. This underlying "intelligence" makes these AI tools important peers of humans in the QA stage of the software development lifecycle. The biggest gain to be reaped from using these tools is that they can apply their intrinsic testing acumen on large codebases in near-real time.

A common frustration is that QA takes a long time, since complex products and extensive codebases usually have hundreds of different user journeys to test, and doing this manually is very time-consuming. Automated tools do not reduce the value of having a human in the loop, but they can certainly automate a lot of repetitive work, freeing human QA professionals to focus on the critical flows, ones that were changed in the last pull request, or whatever makes up the 20% of work that has 80% of the impact (as per the Pareto principle (*https://oreil.ly/qCXc5*), so often used in software development).

Many of the prominent tools I evaluate in this chapter combine functional and nonfunctional testing abilities, as they aim to integrate into various development environments. These tools can be used in different ways, depending on each team's context and preferences. For instance, testing is one of the most significant aspects of the CI/CD process. Thanks to CI/CD-integrated testing tools, we now conduct tests continuously during development rather than waiting until after development. This continuous integration approach provides real-time feedback about your software's performance and internal functioning.

CI/CD-integrated AI testing tools automatically test changes made to your code after every build. Continuous testing ensures that issues are identified and addressed early in the development cycle, reducing the risk of defects in production. This approach promotes a culture of quality and allows for faster, more reliable software releases.

In contrast, browser and cloud-based tools run tests in web browsers or the cloud, providing flexibility and accessibility. They allow testing on different devices and environments, without complex setups like IDEs and CI/CD-integrated tools.

Use Cases

Software developers and engineering teams across various industries are integrating AI testing and QA tools into their processes. Here are some of the prominent use cases that we've seen:

Automated test creation
: Building test automations used to be very slow and time-consuming. It takes a lot of time and mental bandwidth to design and write test scripts, run regression tests, and do everything in between. This is what many AI-driven testing tools aim to help with, by generating comprehensive test scripts from plain English prompts within seconds. This natural language processing (NLP) method of scripting makes it easy to automate complex workflows. This, in turn, makes testing accessible to both technical and nontechnical stakeholders. AI-generated test scripts are usually based on user behavior and existing patterns in previous test data, which makes the tests more relevant and closer to what a human QA tester would create.

Improved test accuracy
: Improving accuracy means fewer code bugs slip through the QA stage to production. AI algorithms' superpower is that, unlike manual testers, they can capture patterns and anomalies at scale. Being trained on extensive codebases and past testing data helps them more easily spot nuances that might indicate an issue requiring the feature to be regressed.

Self-healing capabilities after encountering errors
: AI testing tools with *self-healing* capabilities automatically detect and fix issues in test scripts when changes in the application's UI or code cause tests to fail. This ensures that all tests remain functional and up to date without manual intervention. Historically, updates are one of the biggest challenges for QA teams, since a change in the UI means many tests written in the past also need to be changed. These AI tools can significantly reduce the maintenance burden on QA teams and make the QA process faster and more reliable.

Faster software-release cycles
: By automating repetitive tasks using AI testing tools, we can speed the release cycle of software applications tenfold. Developers can concentrate more of their time on innovating new features and enhancing the product instead of spending the entire day trying to catch bugs or write test scripts. Companies can also respond faster to market demands and user feedback.

The Need for Human Testers

It is important to remember that while these AI tools can do a great job catching issues and bugs that would eventually break production, the human instinct is still crucial during testing. This is not just about the limitations of the tools reviewed here, nor their underlying AI algorithms. It goes beyond that. Software development teams don't write 100% of their requirements and edge cases in an absolutely perfect way.

I can speak from my own experience leading software teams for more than a decade: there are *always* changes and caveats based on last-minute user feedback, an ad hoc request from sales, or even a phone call from the CEO with a specific exception. While teams try hard to properly document all requirements and capture edge cases and test plans in the software development task descriptions, the result is never perfect. There are gaps. And because these are the written materials on which AI tools are trained, and they take project requirements as the ultimate instructions to test against, they'll eventually miss some nuances of those requirements or ad hoc exceptions.

Even beyond that, frankly, there's often specific context awareness that only humans can have. We need humans in order to adapt to industry-wide events or sensitive user concerns. Software development is a complex matter, and the more extensive a product and codebase are, the more likely it is that a purely AI-driven QA process will show its limitations and gaps.

AI algorithms are only as good as the data used in training them. They can absolutely help a lot, as this chapter shows—especially with the repetitive grunt work, like testing an extensive list of user journeys and application flows. But human monitoring, review, and intervention are still needed for the critical parts of the process.

Evaluation Process

Most companies in the QA automation space cater to enterprise clients. This makes sense, given that enterprise companies tend to have larger teams, more extensive products, and much higher quality-control standards. While this is totally fine and expected, it affected my selection process for tools to showcase here, since I gave preference to tools that can be accessed via a simple self-service sign-up process and that offer a free trial. This is a deliberate choice to make it easier for readers to act on what they read here, though it certainly leaves out some tools that required me to speak with their sales teams to negotiate a price package. I decided those tools were out of scope for this book.

Even with that limitation, as I researched this chapter, I reviewed more than 20 automated testing tools (many of which fell into that enterprise sales category). I shortlisted the two tools highlighted next.

To evaluate and compare AI-powered testing tools for this chapter, I used each tool to write and run test cases for a simple, straightforward test site (*https://katalon-demo-cura.herokuapp.com*): a basic web application for booking appointments with a medical doctor. Since developing a comprehensive, end-to-end automated testing framework is a substantial undertaking, I focused on evaluating the specific AI features these testing tools offer, to demonstrate their potential for integrating AI into software testing.

The examples in this book are not intended to represent a complete testing framework, but rather to demonstrate how to use AI-integrated features in automated testing tools. The primary objective of this chapter is to showcase AI's possibilities and simplicity in the software testing domain, not to provide a production-ready solution.

I evaluated how the AI features in these tools enhance various aspects of the testing process, such as generating test cases, creating test data, executing tests, and analyzing results.

Test site
: *https://katalon-demo-cura.herokuapp.com*

App description
: Web app with a login page for booking appointments with a medical doctor

Test description
: Automate a series of actions on a healthcare service website. This test ensures that a patient can navigate the app and use it to successfully book an appointment to meet with the doctor. We want to see if everything works as it should on the app.

Steps
: We intend to generate/create test cases that automatically evaluate whether:

  - The login page works perfectly
  - Users can successfully book appointments if all the required fields are updated
  - The booking history records every booking made

Test case 1

1. Navigate to *https://katalon-demo-cura.herokuapp.com*.
2. Click on the Make Appointment button.
3. Set the text John Doe in the username field.
4. Set encrypted text in the password field.
5. Click on the Login button.
6. Check if the user can successfully log in when the correct information is entered.

Test case 2

On the Make Appointment page:

1. Select a Visit Date.
2. Select the Medicare option.
3. Select the "Apply for hospital readmission" option.
4. Enter a comment in the text area.
5. Book an appointment.
6. Check that the user can successfully book an appointment 10 seconds after submitting the booking form with all the correct information.

Test case 3

1. Toggle the menu.
2. Access the history page by clicking on History.
3. Confirm that the appointment just booked appears in the history.

Now, let's examine the top-performing AI testing tools I found and see how they followed these instructions and evaluated the website using their AI features.

Katalon Studio

Katalon Studio (*https://oreil.ly/xREhC*), launched by Katalon Inc. in 2015, is an automated software QA tool that supports testing for mobile applications, web apps, desktop apps, and APIs. The company's website highlights that it has "embedded AI across our entire platform to test faster, see clearer, and streamline test automation with fewer bottlenecks."

Katalon Studio was the first tool in Katalon's ecosystem. Since then, two additional tools have been added. Katalon Recorder is a browser automation extension for creating and running Firefox, Edge, and Chrome tests. Katalon TestOps is a test-orchestration platform that centralizes test planning and management activities, streamlining DevOps processes and enhancing cross-team collaboration.

The AI-augmented testing features in Katalon include:

- Generating Groovy code from plain English instructions (Groovy is the scripting language used for writing test cases in Katalon)
- Automatically generating test scripts based on prompts
- A Virtual Data Analyst feature that analyzes all your TestOps data and generates reports
- Self-healing capabilities

Katalon's self-healing AI, as noted previously, automatically helps you fix tests that break during runs. You don't have to manually maintain existing test scripts when you ship a new feature or change a component. Regression test plans are also handled automatically: the AI engine instantly reruns your existing functional and nonfunctional tests to ensure that your software's previously developed and tested components still perform correctly even after you've added new changes.

To create test cases in Katalon, you typically either record tests and playback or write test scripts with Groovy.

Practical example

In this example, I used StudioAssist AI, Katalon's generative AI, which helps programmers write test cases from plain-language prompts. I used it to write test cases for the healthcare service website. For the sake of this test, I acted as a stakeholder who doesn't know the Groovy syntax. I used the StudioAssist AI feature in Katalon to generate Groovy scripts, which set up my tests. I wrote the test I wanted in the prompt, and it created a test script for me in Groovy, which I then ran to evaluate the software. StudioAssist also helps explain the function of each line of code it generates.

I created a new test project, set up a test folder, and navigated to the script tab to begin writing my tests. Here is the prompt I gave StudioAssist AI:

Prompt:

```
I want to write a test case performing the following steps:
1. Open the browser to https://katalon-demo-cura.herokuapp.com
2. Click the make appointment button named
'Page_CuraHomepage/btn_MakeAppointment'
3. Fill username in the 'Page_Login/txt_Username' object with the value
in the 'Username' variable
4. Fill the password in the Page_Login/txt_Password' object with the
value in the 'Password' variable
5. Verify that the appointment div 'Page_CuraAppointment/div_Appointment'
exists within 10 seconds.
6. Close the browser
```

Katalon StudioAssist generated test cases written in the correct Groovy syntax (see it in full in Example 4-1) that executed the test script when it was run (see Figures 4-1, 4-2, and 4-3).

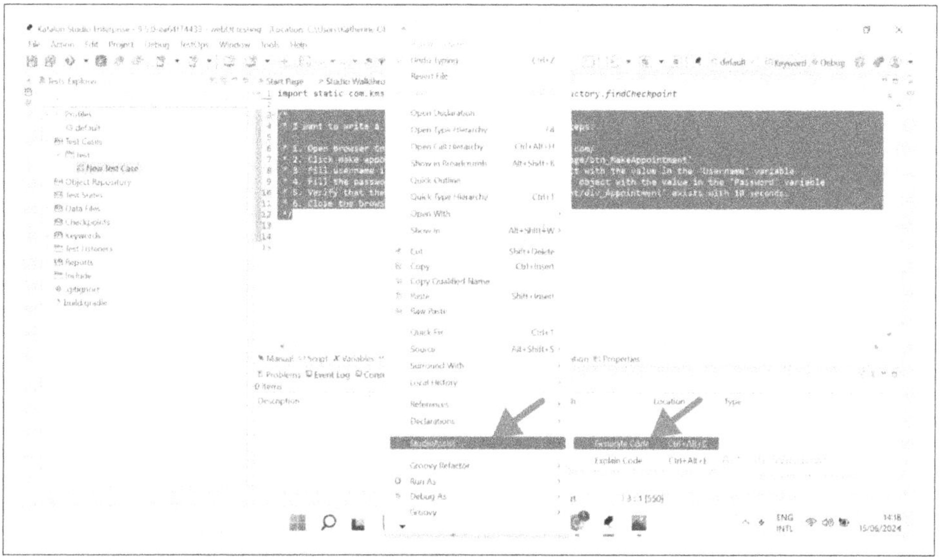

Figure 4-1. Generating tests with Katalon is intuitive when using the StudioAssist option in the UI

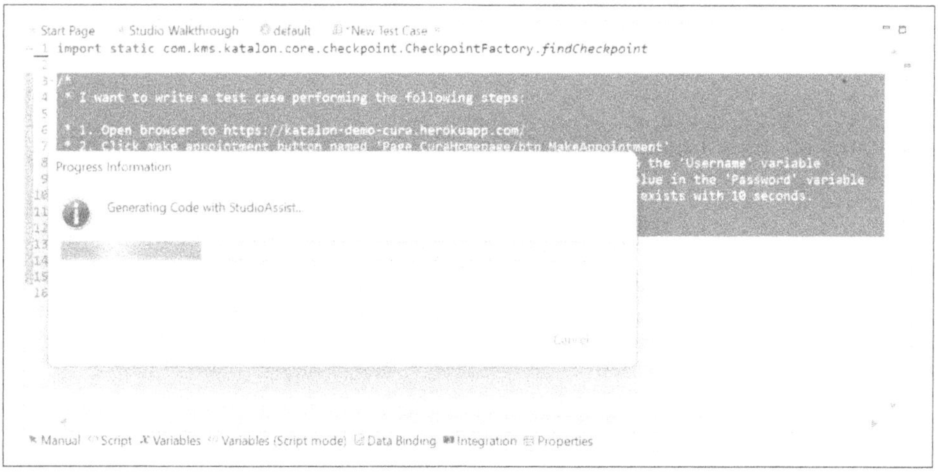

Figure 4-2. Generating tests with Katalon takes a few seconds

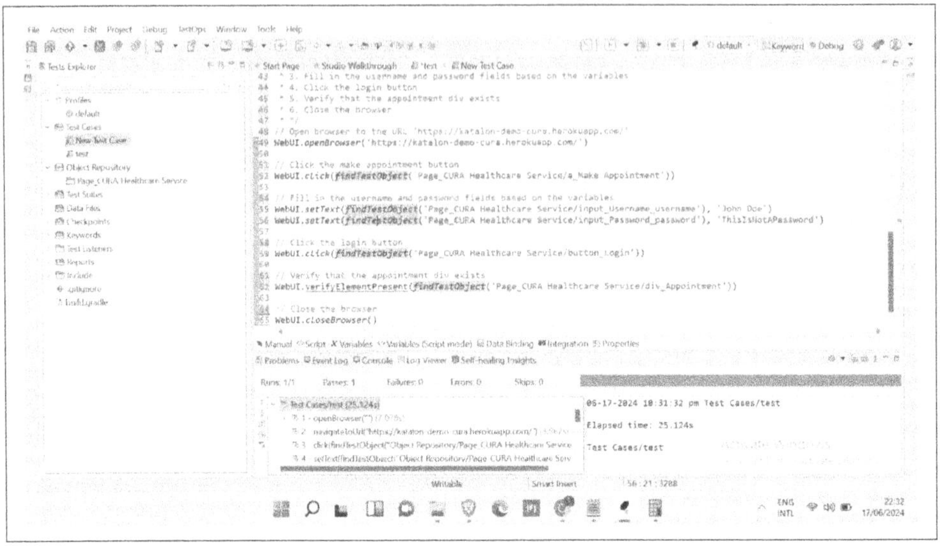

Figure 4-3. Tests generated by Katalon and executed on the StudioAssist UI

Example 4-1. Full code of the tests generated by Katalon

```
/* I want to write a Katalon Studio test case to perform the following steps.
* 1. Open browser to the URL  'https://katalon-demo-cura.herokuapp.com/'
* 2. Click the make appointment button
* 3. Fill in the username and password fields based on the variables
* 4. Click the login button
* 5. Verify that the appointment div exists
* 6. Close the browser
* */
// Open browser to the URL 'https://katalon-demo-cura.herokuapp.com/'
WebUI.openBrowser('https://katalon-demo-cura.herokuapp.com/')

// Click the make appointment button
WebUI.click(findTestObject('Page_CURA Healthcare Service/a_Make Appointment'))

// Fill in the username and password fields based on the variables
WebUI.setText(findTestObject('Page_CURA Healthcare Service/input_Username_username'),
                             'John Doe')
WebUI.setText(findTestObject('Page_CURA Healthcare Service/input_Password_password'),
                             'ThisIsNotAPassword')

// Click the login button
WebUI.click(findTestObject('Page_CURA Healthcare Service/button_Login'))

// Verify that the appointment div exists
WebUI.verifyElementPresent(
      findTestObject('Page_CURA Healthcare Service/div_Appointment'))
```

```
// Close the browser
WebUI.closeBrowser()
```

As you can see, the generated test fulfills the instructions I provided, and the code is written in the correct syntax.

Pros

- StudioAssist is easy for nontechnical users to use and debug, since it transforms natural-language prompts into the correct Groovy testing syntax.
- Built-in keywords and templates speed up the test-creation process and reduce the need for extensive coding.
- Its self-healing capabilities automatically update test scripts when there are changes to the application's UI.
- StudioAssist integrates with popular CI/CD tools and testing frameworks like Jenkins, Git, and Jira.

Cons

- Katalon requires you to download and install StudioAssist (shown in the preceding screenshots). This adds some additional setup work.
- Katalon can sometimes be slow, particularly when dealing with large test suites or complex test scenarios.
- There is a bit of a learning curve with the Katalon StudioAssist UI. Some options are buried inside the cascade options from the top bar, and you'll need to learn keyboard shortcuts.

I rate Katalon a 9 out of 10. It helps a lot with writing tests from plain English text prompts and executing them against the application I want to test, both within the same UI. The only reason I won't rate it 10/10 is the learning curve pointed out in the cons list. It could certainly be more intuitive, although this is a typical UX for complex enterprise products, which Katalon already is.

Let's turn now to the second tool.

testRigor

The next tool I tested is testRigor (*https://oreil.ly/OM9lJ*), an AI-driven automated tool designed to streamline software testing. Unlike traditional testing tools, testRigor allows developers to create and execute tests without writing code. Its NLP capabilities allow you to describe your application's functionality in plain English. The AI then generates, executes, and reports on test cases, significantly reducing the time and technical expertise required for comprehensive software testing.

Practical example

In my evaluation of testRigor, one feature that really stood out was its completely codeless test-creation process. I did not have to write a single line of test code. Instead, I provided my test site URL and a brief description of my application and how it should behave. I also provided my test goals and specified the number of test cases to generate. The AI handled everything, from generating tests to executing them to generating a detailed test report (see Figures 4-4 and 4-5).

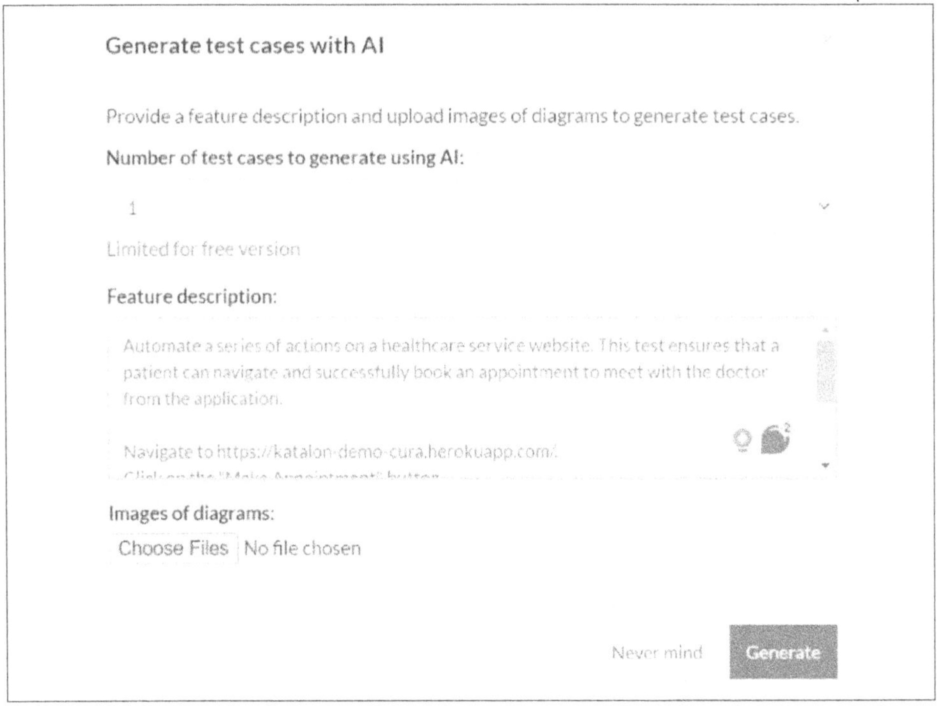

Figure 4-4. Prompt and description to generate test case

Figure 4-5. Tests were executed against the testing app and passed successfully

The goal of the testing, as you may recall, was to check whether a user can log in in less than 10 seconds and successfully book an appointment.

Pros

- testRigor uses Behavior-Driven Test Case Creation, which allows for the creation of tests based on how users interact with the application. This bypasses the technicalities of testing syntax, which can prevent attrition for nontechnical users or smaller teams.
- testRigor's testing product is very accessible, which makes it stand out from the crowd. It's fully cloud-based, which eliminates the need to install additional software (unlike Katalon). This makes it easy to access and use from anywhere.
- It integrates with popular CI/CD pipelines like Jenkins and CircleCI and supports bug-tracking tools like Jira, which make it seamless to integrate with the tools that teams are already using.
- The self-healing functionality, just like Katalon's, reduces the maintenance burden on the testing team whenever existing application workflows are changed.

Cons

- Bypassing actual test writing is great for smaller teams and occasional users, but I doubt it would be practical for larger teams that already have a large testing infrastructure in place. For those software teams (which are the majority), the value of automated testing is to generate the tests in correct syntax.
- A cascade con of this bypass is that testRigor doesn't offer the same flexibility and control as traditional testing languages and frameworks. It would not work well for complex test scenarios or extensive application workflows.

Due to these limitations, I rate testRigor a 7 out of 10. Beyond that, it's a great UX that "just works," and it's a perfect fit for smaller teams that don't have a complex testing infrastructure in place already, or teams whose testing needs are occasional and who just want to check that the product is working as per the requirements.

Tool Comparison

Katalon and testRigor have strengths that cater to different testing needs, though both leverage AI and machine learning to enhance their functionalities. Table 4-1 provides a comparison.

Katalon
: Katalon offers a robust suite of features designed to handle complex test scenarios. It is particularly useful for large-scale testing projects where comprehensive test coverage is critical, and for software development teams that already have a testing infrastructure, team, and processes in place. While the learning curve is steeper than with testRigor, Katalon's depth of features and flexibility in handling diverse testing requirements make it a powerful tool for a larger number of software development teams, especially larger ones or those working on complex products.

testRigor
: I was impressed with testRigor's simplicity and ease of use. The learning curve is notably short, and I found it remarkable how fast I went from signup to actual test results. This tool excels in environments where product features change frequently, requiring rapid and continuous testing. I'd say testRigor is best suited for startup teams or occasional one-off users who don't have an existing testing infrastructure in place and whose product requirements may change too often for them to even set up such a robust testing environment. On the other hand, testRigor poses limitations for those teams where Katalon excels; that is, for larger teams and more complex product workflows.

Table 4-1. AI testing tools overview

Tool	UX	Test performance
Katalon	Repository	9/10
testRigor	Browser	7/10

Conclusion

Of the tools analyzed in this chapter, Katalon emerged as a good pick for larger teams and enterprise products, while testRigor proved to be a winner for startups and side products. That covers the software-development market nicely, and showcases how teams with different types of products and levels of maturity can benefit from using AI testing tools.

If you've ever worked in software testing or QA, or if you've simply written unit tests for any code you wrote, you'll know how laborious it is to write tests and keep them updated as an application evolves and gets extended.

I've often been part of conversations about budget planning and roadmap discussions where robust testing was postponed, or outdated tests were simply framed as technical debt that should be phased out. It's very common for both technical and nontechnical stakeholders to have biases against proper testing practices, and one of the key reasons for that is how significant an investment it has been, historically, to have them.

That brings us to the bulk of the value that AI testing tools can bring to the table. In software development, we're constantly looking for occurrences of the Pareto principle: "What's the 20% of effort that will return 80% of this roadmap item's value?" As a CTO, I've been in the center of these discussions many times. In QA, the 20% of effort that creates 80% of value involves defining the application workflow properly; talking with users and clients about the issues and edge cases; going the extra mile to map out nuances for the software developers who will implement the requirements; and, ultimately, conducting user acceptance testing as a final gatekeeper before going live.

The other 80% of effort, which creates 20% of value, is the actual grunt work of writing and executing each test to verify if the code fulfills the requirements. AI tools excel at this task. Being able to provide instructions in natural language and get back tests written in proper syntax, ready to execute, is a huge time-saving use case. Having those self-healing capabilities to update tests whenever application code is changed is a great backstop for when tests become deprecated and are simply commented out, as pressing priorities emerge to get a release to production.

These are the day-to-day decisions that so often relegate proper software testing to a second-order priority. AI tools can help alleviate those concerns and contribute to ensuring that software running in production is properly tested and bug-free. This can't be done by AI tools *alone*, since these tools won't replace humans. Quite the opposite: the human tasks in QA are critical, as they define the scope of testing and serve as key guidelines for the AI tools to do the grunt work at a high quality standard.

Once again, "AI + human" is a combination that improves an often-frustrating process to produce a higher-quality output.

CHAPTER 5

Predictive Analytics and Performance Optimization

In today's software-driven world, businesses generate vast amounts of data from their applications, users, and operations. This data holds valuable insights that can be used to make decisions, predict trends, and improve system performance. The ability to analyze and act on this data has become a critical skill for software engineers.

In this chapter, I tap into data analytics and business intelligence, and I'll test how state-of-the-art AI tools can help businesses understand their data and improve their results. Whether it's predicting future user behavior or optimizing resource usage, data analytics opens up new possibilities. Here are three key angles this chapter will cover:

Analyzing data
: The first promise these tools make is that users can query large datasets by asking questions in natural language. This seems attractive, given how costly it is for companies to build visualization dashboards on top of their databases.

Distilling advanced insights
: Companies often want to correlate data points and find patterns in order to understand user behavior or spot some malfunction in their processes, in ways that go well beyond simply querying the data to count and sum fields. Again, the costs of such projects prevent many companies from even stepping into this territory, so the promise of AI tools removing this barrier is a big one.

Predicting future behavior
: The ultimate promise of data science and business intelligence is to pick up data about what happened in the past and use it to draw conclusions about what will happen in the near future. This forecasting can be a game-changer for businesses that do it well, and the companies that develop and use it as a key part of their decision-making processes treat these projects and algorithms as sensitive intellectual property.

These angles show how software engineers and data analysts can turn raw data into actionable insights to help teams make smarter decisions. They also show how expensive and time-consuming these projects have been, historically. High costs and complexity have limited sophisticated projects in these fields to companies that have the funds and the technically capable teams to drive them. Most small to medium businesses, startups, and nontech businesses face high barriers to developing such tools, which hinders their ability to compete in this global market. The promise of AI tools in this sector is to democratize access to such tools among all market participants, regardless of their size, sector, or the technical abilities of their teams.

Before we look at the tools themselves, let's quickly review a few data analysis basics.

Data Collection and Sources

At the heart of data analytics is the data itself. In software engineering, this data comes from many sources, such as:

User activity
: Information about how users interact with software, including page views, click paths, and session lengths

System logs
: Detailed records of system and application performance, which help engineers monitor health and performance

Tracking tools
: Automatically collected real-time data on application performance, such as response times and error rates

Customer feedback
: Insights from user reviews, support tickets, and surveys, providing a qualitative perspective on user satisfaction

Market research
: Competitive analysis, news, market reports, and all relevant information that's published every day

There's a long tail of other possible sources of valuable data that businesses can use to shape their decisions about the future. These data sources form the foundation of data analysis. They also shape the quality of the data and determine how much data cleaning is required. For example, if a dataset contains lots of empty fields or inconsistent field types, it takes significant specialized work to clean the dataset for analysis, as well as advanced techniques like data normalization and clustering. I'll be exploring these techniques in the tools analyzed in this chapter.

Use Cases for Data Analytics

With valuable data in hand, data analysts can tackle a variety of challenges. We'll tap into some of these key use cases for data analysis and business intelligence in the tool evaluation section of this chapter.

Performance insights
: By analyzing system metrics and logs, engineers can identify performance bottlenecks and inefficiencies early on. This helps in optimizing resource usage, improving response times, and ensuring the application remains scalable as demand grows. For example, tracking CPU and memory usage over time can reveal patterns that signal when a system needs scaling or optimization.

User behavior prediction
: Data analytics can uncover patterns in user behavior, helping teams anticipate future user needs and preferences. By analyzing user activity data, such as click paths and session lengths, engineers can predict which features users will likely use more and tailor their product development efforts accordingly. This allows teams to focus on enhancements that will have the most impact on user satisfaction and engagement.

Capacity planning
: Analyzing historical usage data can help teams predict future resource needs and scale infrastructure appropriately to meet demand. By understanding traffic patterns, engineers can forecast peak usage periods and prepare systems to handle higher loads without compromising performance.

Anomaly detection
: Automated systems can analyze operational data to detect unusual patterns that could signal potential security breaches, system failures, or fraudulent activity. This proactive approach allows engineers to address issues before they escalate, minimizing downtime and protecting user data.

Business intelligence

Beyond performance and system optimization, data analytics can offer broader insights into business performance. This includes tracking product adoption, analyzing market trends, and evaluating key business metrics. These insights help guide strategic decisions, such as which new features to prioritize or how to allocate resources more effectively.

Each of these use cases highlights how data analytics allows teams to make informed decisions, optimize processes, and improve both software performance and the overall business strategy. The sections that follow look at how to approach these use cases with the right tools, models, and techniques. We'll also explore how AI and machine learning can further enhance data analytics, helping engineers automate processes and uncover insights faster.

Types of AI Tools for Data Analysis

AI tools have been emerging in data analysis, as they have in many other industries and verticals. Just using many enterprise tools requires complex sales and onboarding processes; I've left those out of the scope of this book, with the goal of steering you toward the most accessible options.

I've also found some tools that offer infrastructure-level support for data analysis. While many of them are valuable, this chapter's use case is about a business owner who wants to extract business-worthy insights from a dataset, and such tools are overkill for such cases.

I ended up with tools that offer self-service onboarding and that have a free tier that allows readers to test the software. Almost all of these tools contain a chatbot UX that lets you upload a data file and ask analytical questions about the data. This seems to be the winning UX pattern for data analysis use cases.

Evaluation Process

I evaluated more than 20 AI tools in the data analysis and business intelligence space in order to shortlist the ones I highlight in this chapter. Every tool covered here meets the following criteria:

- It is a professional project with a competent team behind it.
- It generates high-quality results.
- It offers some level of functionality for free or on a trial basis.
- It has a high level of adoption at the time of writing (mid-2025).

For this test I'm using a public dataset of one year of online retail transactions (*https://oreil.ly/trSz7*) from the Machine Learning Repository at the University of California, Irvine. It contains over 500,000 transactions, with eight data columns for each transaction:

- InvoiceNo
- StockCode
- Description
- Quantity
- InvoiceDate
- UnitPrice
- CustomerID
- Country

You can see a sample in Figure 5-1.

InvoiceNo	StockCode	Description	Quantity	InvoiceDate	UnitPrice	CustomerID	Country
536365	85123A	WHITE HANGING HEART T-LIGHT HOLDER	6	12/1/10 8:26	2.55	17850	United Kingdom
536365	71053	WHITE METAL LANTERN	6	12/1/10 8:26	3.39	17850	United Kingdom
536365	84406B	CREAM CUPID HEARTS COAT HANGER	8	12/1/10 8:26	2.75	17850	United Kingdom
536365	84029G	KNITTED UNION FLAG HOT WATER BOTTLE	6	12/1/10 8:26	3.39	17850	United Kingdom
536365	84029E	RED WOOLLY HOTTIE WHITE HEART.	6	12/1/10 8:26	3.39	17850	United Kingdom
536365	22752	SET 7 BABUSHKA NESTING BOXES	2	12/1/10 8:26	7.65	17850	United Kingdom
536365	21730	GLASS STAR FROSTED T-LIGHT HOLDER	6	12/1/10 8:26	4.25	17850	United Kingdom
536366	22633	HAND WARMER UNION JACK	6	12/1/10 8:28	1.85	17850	United Kingdom
536366	22632	HAND WARMER RED POLKA DOT	6	12/1/10 8:28	1.85	17850	United Kingdom

Figure 5-1. Sample of the online retail transactions dataset

For this comparison test, I'll act as if I'm the owner of an online retailer and attempt to use the AI tools to draw business-worthy insights from this data. I'll ask questions like:

- What are my top-selling products?
- Which of my customer segments have the highest lifetime value?
- What is my sales forecast for the following year?

In this test, I'm importing the raw dataset into each tool, working through the UX to get insights, and taking note of the results I get, how easy it is to get them, and how the tools compare to each other.

Julius

Julius AI (*https://julius.ai*) automates complex data analysis processes and provides interpretations, visualizations, and predictive analytics. It uses a combination of OpenAI's GPT-4 and Anthropic's Claude as its underlying data-processing models.

Julius's instant-messaging UI (Figure 5-2) resembles those of ChatGPT and other popular AI tools. I used it to upload my dataset, then asked my first question, in natural language:

```
What are the top selling products, both by number of units and by
revenue generated?
```

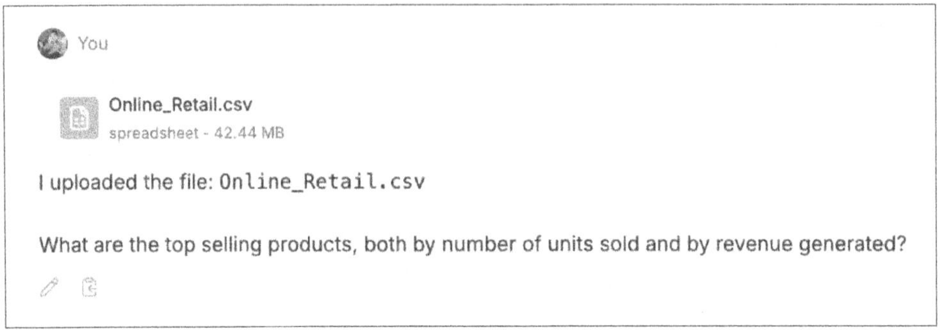

You
Online_Retail.csv
spreadsheet - 42.44 MB
I uploaded the file: Online_Retail.csv
What are the top selling products, both by number of units sold and by revenue generated?

Figure 5-2. My file upload and first prompt to Julius

Julius took just over a minute to run several Python scripts, then returned the tables shown in Figures 5-3 and 5-4, which list the 10 top-selling products by number of units sold and by revenue generated.

Top 10 Products by Units Sold:

Optional: Click on columns or rows to focus on specific data — Export

	Quantity
WORLD WAR 2 GLIDERS ASSTD DESIGNS	53847
JUMBO BAG RED RETROSPOT	47363
ASSORTED COLOUR BIRD ORNAMENT	36381
POPCORN HOLDER	36334
PACK OF 72 RETROSPOT CAKE CASES	36039
WHITE HANGING HEART T-LIGHT HOLDER	35317
RABBIT NIGHT LIGHT	30680
MINI PAINT SET VINTAGE	26437
PACK OF 12 LONDON TISSUES	26315
PACK OF 60 PINK PAISLEY CAKE CASES	24753

Figure 5-3. Part of Julius's reply to the first prompt, showing the top-selling products by quantity

Top 10 Products by Revenue:

Optional: Click on columns or rows to focus on specific data

Export

	TotalRevenue
DOTCOM POSTAGE	206245.48
REGENCY CAKESTAND 3 TIER	164762.19
WHITE HANGING HEART T-LIGHT HOLDER	99668.47
PARTY BUNTING	98302.98
JUMBO BAG RED RETROSPOT	92356.03
RABBIT NIGHT LIGHT	66756.59
POSTAGE	66230.64
PAPER CHAIN KIT 50'S CHRISTMAS	63791.94
ASSORTED COLOUR BIRD ORNAMENT	58959.73
CHILLI LIGHTS	53768.06

Figure 5-4. Part of Julius's reply to the first prompt, showing the top-selling products by revenue

Along with the hard data, Julius offered some contextual explanation about high-value products (Figure 5-5), highlighting some interesting aspects of the data.

Key observations:

1. Units Sold: The top-selling product by quantity is "WORLD WAR 2 GLIDERS ASSTD DESIGNS" with 53,847 units sold, followed by "JUMBO BAG RED RETROSPOT" with 47,363 units.

2. Revenue Generated: The product generating the highest revenue is "DOTCOM POSTAGE" with £206,245.48, followed by "REGENCY CAKESTAND 3 TIER" with £164,762.19.

3. Overlap: Some products appear in both lists, indicating they are popular in terms of both quantity sold and revenue generated. For example, "WHITE HANGING HEART T-LIGHT HOLDER" and "JUMBO BAG RED RETROSPOT" are in both top 10 lists.

4. Interesting Notes:

   - "DOTCOM POSTAGE" is the highest revenue generator but doesn't appear in the top 10 by units sold, suggesting it's a high-value, low-volume item.
   - Some low-cost, high-volume items like "PACK OF 72 RETROSPOT CAKE CASES" appear in the top units sold but not in the top revenue list.

This analysis provides insights into which products are most popular and which are most profitable, which can be valuable for inventory management and marketing strategies.

Figure 5-5. Some of Julius's observations about the data in response to the first prompt

Next, I asked Julius to identify which customer segments were generating the highest value for this online retail store:

```
From the same dataset, do customer segmentation and calculate lifetime
value of each client segment. I want to identify the highest value
customer segments.
```

Julius decided to follow the Recency, Frequency, Monetary (RFM) method (*https://oreil.ly/Dm0QZ*) and ran some Python scripts again for almost two minutes, then presented the customer clusters and their lifetime value (Figure 5-6).

The highest value customer segment is Cluster 3. This segment is characterized by:

- Very recent purchases (Recency: 1 day)
- Extremely high purchase frequency (5,914 purchases)
- High monetary value (£64,776.60 spent)
- Exceptionally high LTV (£13,982,742,192.25)

Key Insights:

1. Cluster 3 represents the most valuable customers. These are likely large business customers or resellers who make very frequent, high-value purchases.
2. Cluster 2 is the second most valuable segment, with very recent, frequent, and high-value purchases.
3. Cluster 0 represents average customers with moderate recency, frequency, and monetary values.
4. Cluster 1 is the least valuable segment, with infrequent, low-value purchases and the longest time since their last purchase.

Figure 5-6. Julius's reply to the second prompt, with its analysis of high-value customers

Julius figured that clients that make an average 5,914 purchases and generate £64k per year are likely to be resellers, and gave me pointers on how to use that information for my marketing efforts. This is a unique and very good insight; however, key information is still missing, such as how large this cluster is and how representative these figures are. Is it an outlier case of an extremely high-value client, or does it include hundreds or even thousands of clients that I can market toward to grow the business?

Also, Julius clearly hallucinated on its lifetime value (LTV) calculation: by no means would any client be worth £13 billion. It's not clear what went wrong, but my hunch is that Julius used the wrong field in this calculation.

My third question about this dataset asked Julius to do some forecasting:

```
Assume I do a marketing investment of £500k to grow this customer
segment that you've identified as high-LTV. Forecast my total sales
volume for the next 12 months, both in units sold and in revenue. I
want to provision inventory based on your forecast. Generate a table
for the 20 top selling products in the forecast, with product name
and quantity to provision for next year.
```

In this forecast (Figure 5-7), Julius first made the fair assumption that these marketing efforts would generate a 20% sales increase. However, note that its total revenue forecast is off: the current year's revenue is around £9.7 million, so this £565k forecast would be a massive decrease.

Based on the analysis of the high-LTV customer segment and the assumed £500k marketing investment, here's the forecast for the next 12 months:

Forecast for the next 12 months:

Total units sold: 373,943

Total revenue: £565,777.18

This forecast assumes a 20% growth in sales and revenue due to the marketing investment targeting the high-LTV customer segment.

Figure 5-7. Part of Julius's reply to the third prompt, with sales forecast

Second, the table it created with the number of items to provision for next year, shown in Figure 5-8, is also off (probably a cascade from the wrong revenue estimation). The quantities listed are way below the current year's sales volume for those items. So, while Julius's forecast indicates a 20% sales increase, its stock-provisioning figures suggest a *decrease* of 60% or more.

	Forecast_Quantity
PACK OF 72 RETROSPOT CAKE CASES	5883
RABBIT NIGHT LIGHT	5830
SPACEBOY LUNCH BOX	5448
DOLLY GIRL LUNCH BOX	4972
JUMBO BAG RED RETROSPOT	3979
ROUND SNACK BOXES SET OF4 WOODLAND	3766
WOODLAND CHARLOTTE BAG	3169
RED TOADSTOOL LED NIGHT LIGHT	3103
RED RETROSPOT CHARLOTTE BAG	2809
JUMBO BAG WOODLAND ANIMALS	2686

Figure 5-8. Part of Julius's reply to the third prompt, with its stock-provisioning forecast

Julius did well in the objective data analysis in the first prompt and showed promise in customer segmentation, where it offered an insightful analysis despite the error in its calculation. However, its forecasting was far off the mark. While this could perhaps be mitigated with some prompt engineering, I believe my question was specific enough that I could reasonably expect a better answer.

As such, I'm rating Julius a 7/10 in this test.

Akkio

Akkio (*https://www.akkio.com*) provides AI-driven data analysis and predictive modeling aimed at digital-marketing and ad-targeting clients. Akkio uses its own model, called AD LLM, which it claims to have trained on advertising-specific data to understand data structures, business requirements, and other context specific to ad targeting.

Akkio's polished UI starts with a file upload, prompting users to select from a number of file formats. Once I uploaded my file, Akkio took some two minutes to fully ingest it and make the product functionality available to me. While the file renders as a spreadsheet table in the UI's Prepare tab, the product offers several different features (Figure 5-9): Prepare, Explore, Predict, Deployments, and Reports.

Figure 5-9. Akkio navigation UI

The Explore tab displays an instant-messaging UI similar to the one in Julius. As such, I began with the same prompt, asking about the top-selling products:

```
What are the top selling products, both by number of units and by revenue
generated?
```

Akkio took just a few seconds to reply to my prompts. However, the output was quite raw and lacked context, often consisting of just a data table, with no accompanying text to provide context. For instance, in response to my first question, it simply returned charts and tables (Figures 5-10 and 5-11) with the top-selling products by quantity and by revenue generated, respectively.

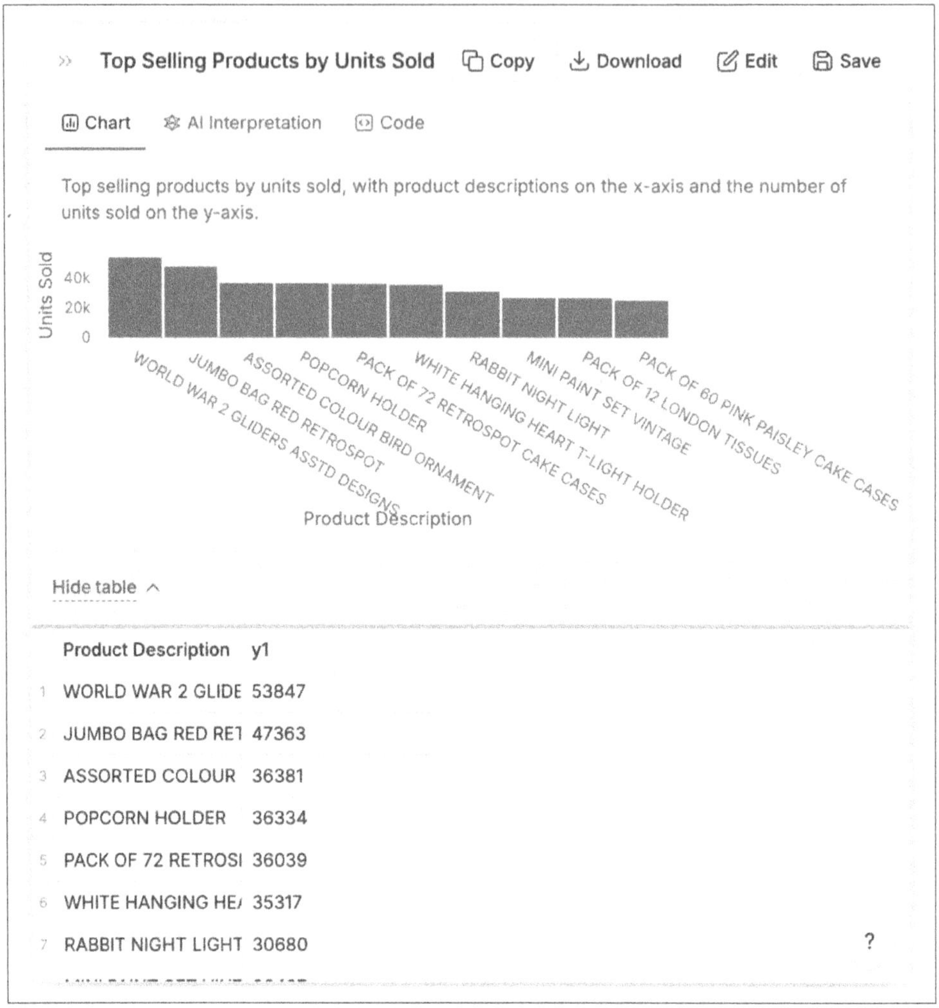

Figure 5-10. Part of Akkio's reply to my first prompt, with top-selling products by quantity

I used the AI Interpretation widget above each chart, but it didn't help much, since the explanation was very technical. It simply described in natural language the technicalities of the query performed against the data; there was no functional context about the analysis being made or what we are seeing in the rendered visualization.

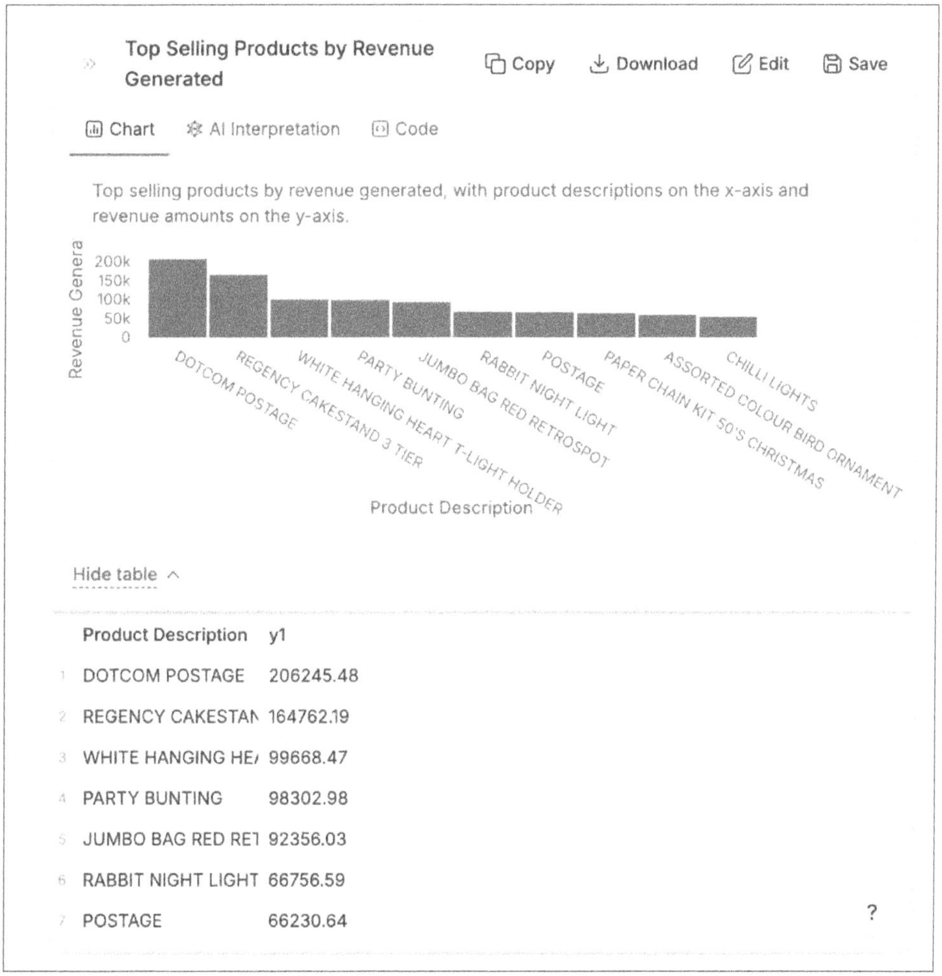

Figure 5-11. Part of Akkio's reply to my first prompt, with top-selling products by revenue

Akkio's response to the first question was correct, so I proceeded to the second question:

```
From the same dataset, do customer segmentation and calculate lifetime
value of each client segment. I want to identify the highest value
customer segments.
```

Akkio's reply is good (see Figure 5-12) since it tells me that the highest-value customer segment is composed of 2,539 clients, who generated an average of about £3,000 each. However, that cluster is too large. I'd expect such a cluster to be perhaps 10% to 20% of the total number of customers, but this one encompasses more than *half* of the 4,372 unique customers in the whole dataset.

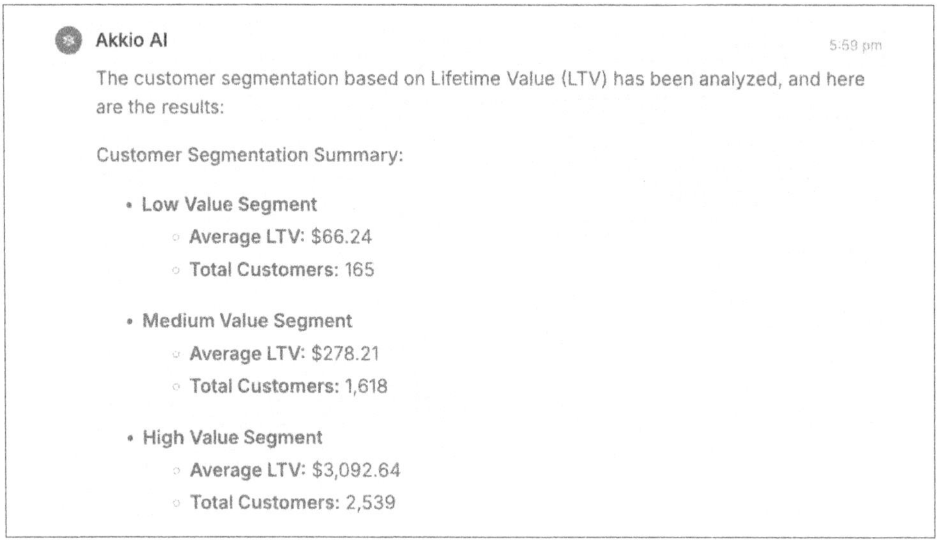

Akkio AI
5:59 pm
The customer segmentation based on Lifetime Value (LTV) has been analyzed, and here are the results:
Customer Segmentation Summary:
Low Value Segment
Average LTV: $66.24
Total Customers: 165
Medium Value Segment
Average LTV: $278.21
Total Customers: 1,618
High Value Segment
Average LTV: $3,092.64
Total Customers: 2,539

Figure 5-12. Part of Akkio's reply to my second prompt, with customer segmentation and value calculations

Working with such a broad cluster of customers produces generic recommendations that aren't very actionable, as seen in Figure 5-13. These recommendations would apply to any business; none of them are specific to high-value customers in a way that I can use for marketing purposes.

Akkio AI 6:00 pm

The **High Value** customer segment consists of clients who spend a lot of money on your products. They are your best customers, contributing significantly to your revenue.

Characteristics of High Value Customers:

1. **Frequent Buyers**: They tend to make multiple purchases, indicating they enjoy your products and come back for more.
2. **Loyalty**: These customers are likely loyal to your brand, as they have already invested a considerable amount of money.
3. **Variety in Purchases**: They may buy a range of products, which shows they are interested in what you offer.

Targeting Strategies for Marketing Campaigns:

1. **Personalized Offers**: Send them special discounts or exclusive offers based on their past purchases to encourage them to buy again.
2. **Loyalty Programs**: Implement a rewards program where they can earn points with each purchase, which can be redeemed for future discounts or gifts.
3. **Feedback and Engagement**: Reach out to them for feedback on new products or services. Engaging them can strengthen their loyalty and make them feel valued.
4. **Exclusive Previews**: Offer them early access to new products or collections, making them feel like VIPs.

Figure 5-13. Part of Akkio's reply to my second prompt, with an explanation about the clients with the highest lifetime value

I proceeded to the third question:

```
Assume I do a marketing investment of £500k to grow this customer segment that
you've identified as high-LTV. Forecast my total sales volume for the next 12
months, both in units sold and in revenue. I want to provision inventory based
on your forecast. Generate a table for the 20 top selling products in the
forecast, with product name and quantity to provision for next year.
```

Akkio's reply is so devoid of context that it's hard to understand the rationale behind the numbers. The revenue figure of £9.8 million (Figure 5-14) is a slight increase over the current year's £9.7 million in revenue, which seems too low given the marketing investment I mentioned in my prompt—but, again, no context is provided for that forecast.

Akkio AI 6:00 pm

Projected Total Revenue for the Next 12 Months: £9815281.35 Projected Total Units Sold for the Next 12 Months: 19958

Figure 5-14. Part of Akkio's reply to my third prompt, with sales forecast

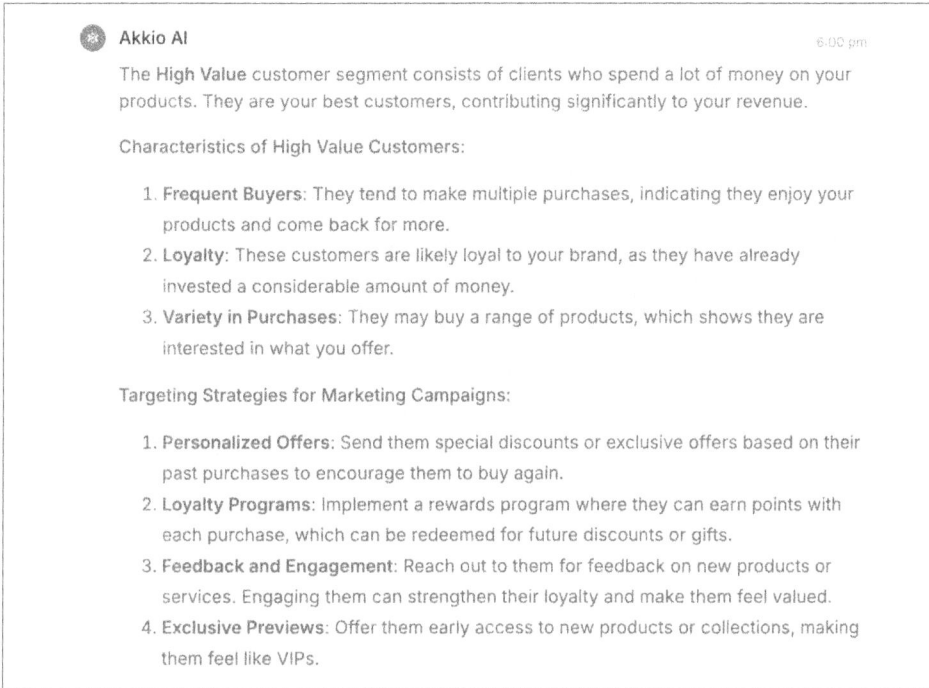

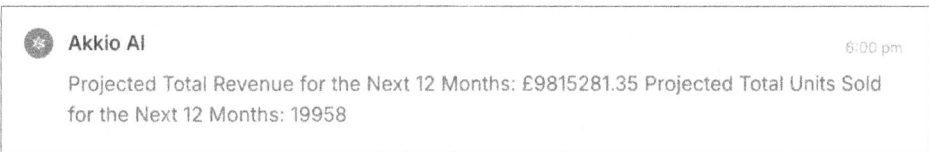

Also, there seems to be some hallucination in the stock-provisioning forecast (Figure 5-15). These numbers are way below the current year's sales for those products, by an order of magnitude. For example, Akkio forecasts 1,918 sales for the first item on the list, even though the current year's sales for that item total 53,847. This, too, suggests some confusion in the calculations, but without any visibility into the scripts or functional explanations of the context, it's hard to understand the process that led to those predictions.

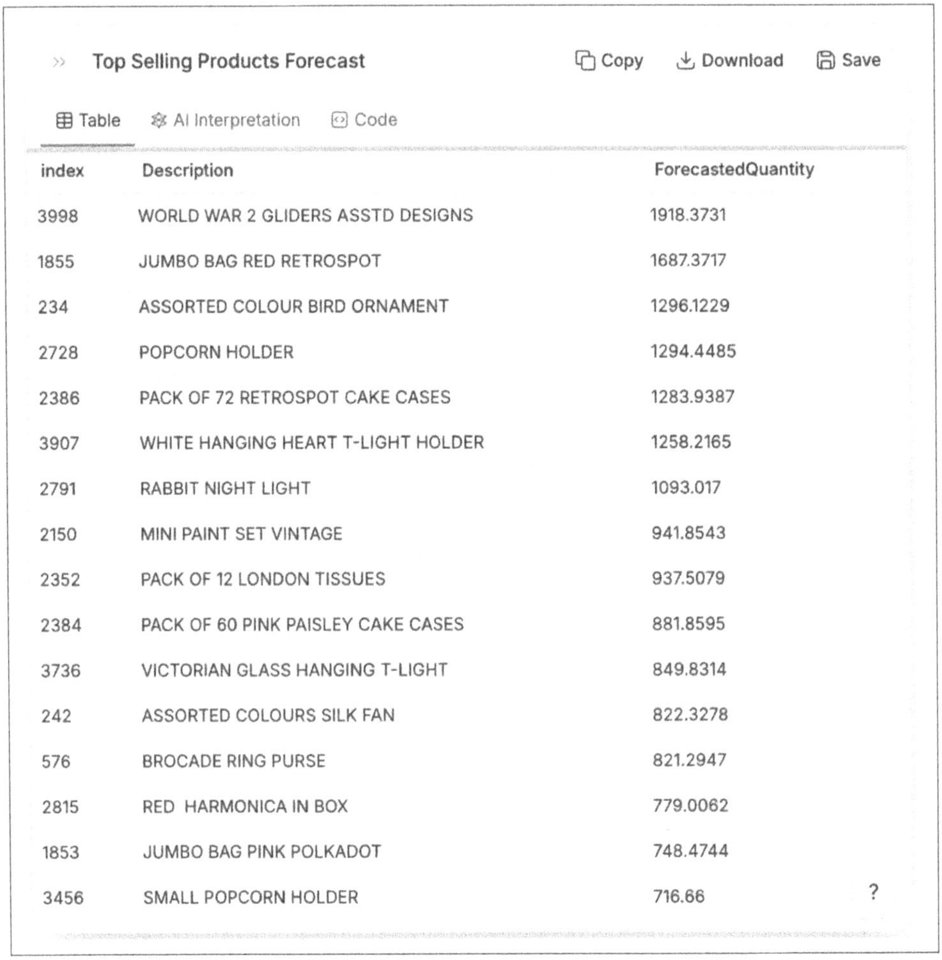

index	Description	ForecastedQuantity
3998	WORLD WAR 2 GLIDERS ASSTD DESIGNS	1918.3731
1855	JUMBO BAG RED RETROSPOT	1687.3717
234	ASSORTED COLOUR BIRD ORNAMENT	1296.1229
2728	POPCORN HOLDER	1294.4485
2386	PACK OF 72 RETROSPOT CAKE CASES	1283.9387
3907	WHITE HANGING HEART T-LIGHT HOLDER	1258.2165
2791	RABBIT NIGHT LIGHT	1093.017
2150	MINI PAINT SET VINTAGE	941.8543
2352	PACK OF 12 LONDON TISSUES	937.5079
2384	PACK OF 60 PINK PAISLEY CAKE CASES	881.8595
3736	VICTORIAN GLASS HANGING T-LIGHT	849.8314
242	ASSORTED COLOURS SILK FAN	822.3278
576	BROCADE RING PURSE	821.2947
2815	RED HARMONICA IN BOX	779.0062
1853	JUMBO BAG PINK POLKADOT	748.4744
3456	SMALL POPCORN HOLDER	716.66

Figure 5-15. Part of Akkio's reply to my third prompt, with product provisioning forecast

Here, too, using the AI Interpretation tab (Figure 5-16) doesn't help much. It provides a technical description of the query used to feed the chart, but it doesn't explain the broader thought process that led to that query.

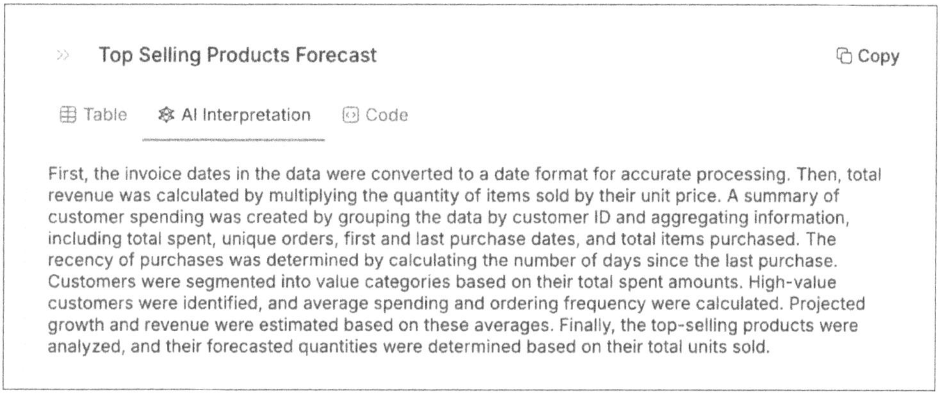

Figure 5-16. AI interpretation of the results

Akkio did well on the objective data analysis with the first prompt, and it did some decent customer segmentation work with the second prompt. However, its forecasting was off. I think the most underwhelming aspect of using Akkio is how little context it provides for its replies. It comes across as a tool best used for simple dataset queries and charts that don't require much analysis or contextualization.

As such, I'm rating Akkio a 5/10.

ChatGPT

Since the top products that emerged in this category offer a chatbot-type experience, I decided to add ChatGPT for comparison, since it is most people's go-to AI tool. I'll quickly review its replies for each of the same three questions.

As seen in Figure 5-17, in reply to my first question, ChatGPT correctly counted the product sales and summed the revenue.

Top Selling Products

		StockCode	Description	total_units_
1	3617	84077	WORLD WAR 2 GLIDERS ASSTD DESIGNS	53847
2	4197	85099B	JUMBO BAG RED RETROSPOT	47363
3	3956	84879	ASSORTED COLOUR BIRD ORNAMENT	36381
4	1333	22197	POPCORN HOLDER	36334
			PACK OF 72	

Top Revenue Generating Products

	StockCode	Description	total_units_sold	total_revenu
1	DOT	DOTCOM POSTAGE	707	206245.48
2	22423	REGENCY CAKESTAND 3 TIER	13033	164762.19
3	47566	PARTY BUNTING	18022	98302.98
4	85123A	WHITE HANGING HEART T-LIGHT HOLDER	35025	97715.99
5	85099B	JUMBO BAG RED RETROSPOT	47363	92356.03

Figure 5-17. ChatGPT's reply to my first prompt

The second question is more nuanced. ChatGPT found a customer segment of 498 generating an LTV of £403,000. However, that value is higher than the revenue generated by *any* client in the current year, which seems to be a mistake. ChatGPT could be assuming that clients will be purchasing for many years into the future, which would inflate the LTV calculations.

When I asked ChatGPT for more details about that highest LTV customer segment, its reply (Figure 5-18) was underwhelming and generic enough to apply to any business, rather than being specific to this dataset and the underlying business.

The highest LTV customer segment, labeled **444**, represents the most valuable clients for your business. Here's what their RFM score means in layman terms:

- **Recency (4)**: These customers have purchased from you very recently, meaning they are still actively engaged with your brand.
- **Frequency (4)**: They buy frequently, showing they have a strong relationship with your products and trust your offerings.
- **Monetary (4)**: These customers spend the most, making high-value purchases, which contributes significantly to your revenue.

Figure 5-18. Part of ChatGPT's reply to my second prompt, with its explanation for the customer segmentation

ChatGPT's reply to my third question, asking it to forecast revenue and stock provisioning based on a significant marketing investment, started off quite well. ChatGPT estimated that the marketing investment would produce a sales increase of 20% to 40% in this customer segment.

However, its product stock-provisioning forecasts are off (Figure 5-19): again, the sales numbers it predicts are lower than the current year's. To me, this suggests that ChatGPT calculated the number of items to be sold *only* to this high-value customer segment and "forgot" to include the items sold to all other clients.

Top 20 Products Forecast For Next Year

	Description	Forecasted_Quantity
1	WORLD WAR 2 GLIDERS ASSTD DESIGNS	39092.3
2	JUMBO BAG RED RETROSPOT	34197.8
3	WHITE HANGING HEART T-LIGHT HOLDER	27166.100000000002
4	POPCORN HOLDER	26920.4
	PACK OF 72	

I have provided a table with the top 20 products and their forecasted quantities based on the projected growth from your marketing investment. This forecast accounts for a 30% increase in sales volume and reflects the quantity you should provision for the next year. Let me know if you'd like to adjust any parameters or dive deeper into specific details!

Figure 5-19. Part of ChatGPT's reply to my third prompt, with product stock-provisioning forecast

ChatGPT did well in the objective data analysis with the first prompt, and it offered a good amount of context and reasoning in response to the other questions, despite some obvious issues with the calculations. I believe some of these issues might be mitigated with prompt engineering. It's also worth noting that ChatGPT isn't really a native data analysis tool: unlike the other tools analyzed here, it renders clunky tables and has no ability to render charts.

As such, I'm rating ChatGPT a 6/10.

Tool Comparison

My first challenge with this comparison is that all three of the tools I analyzed were subject to a black-box effect. I input a large volume of data, and within seconds these tools output good-looking tables, charts, and write-ups with conclusions and insights that appear to make sense. It would be easy to assume that the information provided by these tools is correct, given their impressive speed and output.

However, I double-checked the results by running a script on my local machine against the reference dataset (Figure 5-20; this script is available in the book's GitHub repository (*https://github.com/sergiopereira-io/oreilly_book*)).

Comparing the tools' results against my local tests, I first observed that all tools *missed* the product with most units sold ("Small Popcorn Holder"). I dug a bit into this quirk, but I couldn't figure out why. I can speculate that, since this item has a very low unit price, perhaps a rounding-to-zero type of error could have caused it to be missed.

Besides that, all tools performed quite similarly, both in terms of the value they provided and their pitfalls. From a UX perspective, Akkio stands out from the other tools. It sets a higher expectation by offering what seems like a very robust process with multiple steps and tools. However, it ends up standing out negatively, because the level of contextualization it provides for each interaction is way below what the other tools offer.

Julius and ChatGPT are simpler chatbot experiences that take longer to reply, but offer insights into what's happening and how my data is being processed. Both of those tools include text in their replies alongside the tables and charts, to provide context and reasoning for their operations and to show users how to read the data and interpret the results.

```
sergiopereira@Sergios-MBP chapter6 % node data_analysis.js
Total number of unique products sold: 4070
Total revenue from all products: £ 9747747.93
Top 30 products by total units sold:
1. SMALL POPCORN HOLDER - 56450 units sold
2. WORLD WAR 2 GLIDERS ASSTD DESIGNS - 53847 units sold
3. JUMBO BAG RED RETROSPOT - 47363 units sold
4. WHITE HANGING HEART T-LIGHT HOLDER - 38830 units sold
5. ASSORTED COLOUR BIRD ORNAMENT - 36221 units sold
6. PACK OF 72 RETROSPOT CAKE CASES - 36039 units sold
7. RABBIT NIGHT LIGHT - 30646 units sold
8. MINI PAINT SET VINTAGE  - 26437 units sold
9. PACK OF 12 LONDON TISSUES  - 26315 units sold
10. PACK OF 60 PINK PAISLEY CAKE CASES - 24753 units sold
11. VICTORIAN GLASS HANGING T-LIGHT - 23854 units sold
12. BROCADE RING PURSE  - 23053 units sold
13. ASSORTED COLOURS SILK FAN - 22552 units sold
14. RED  HARMONICA IN BOX  - 22066 units sold
15. JUMBO BAG PINK POLKADOT - 21009 units sold
16. mailout - 20013 units sold
17. LUNCH BAG RED RETROSPOT - 18979 units sold
18. ANTIQUE SILVER TEA GLASS ETCHED - 18911 units sold
19. PAPER CHAIN KIT 50'S CHRISTMAS  - 18902 units sold
20. 60 TEATIME FAIRY CAKE CASES - 18040 units sold
21. PARTY BUNTING - 18022 units sold
22. CHARLOTTE BAG SUKI DESIGN - 18003 units sold
23. HEART OF WICKER SMALL - 17791 units sold
24. RED RETROSPOT CHARLOTTE BAG - 17548 units sold
25. COLOUR GLASS T-LIGHT HOLDER HANGING - 16380 units sold
26. GROW A FLYTRAP OR SUNFLOWER IN TIN - 16172 units sold
27. JAM MAKING SET PRINTED - 16081 units sold
28. JUMBO BAG STRAWBERRY - 16035 units sold
29. 60 CAKE CASES VINTAGE CHRISTMAS - 15767 units sold
30. PACK OF 72 SKULL CAKE CASES - 15128 units sold
Top 30 products by total revenue:
1. DOTCOM POSTAGE - £206245.48 in revenue
2. REGENCY CAKESTAND 3 TIER - £164762.19 in revenue
3. PARTY BUNTING - £98302.98 in revenue
4. WHITE HANGING HEART T-LIGHT HOLDER - £97894.50 in revenue
5. JUMBO BAG RED RETROSPOT - £92356.03 in revenue
6. RABBIT NIGHT LIGHT - £66756.59 in revenue
7. POSTAGE - £66230.64 in revenue
8. PAPER CHAIN KIT 50'S CHRISTMAS  - £63791.94 in revenue
9. ASSORTED COLOUR BIRD ORNAMENT - £58959.73 in revenue
10. CHILLI LIGHTS - £53768.06 in revenue
11. PICNIC BASKET WICKER SMALL - £51041.37 in revenue
12. SMALL POPCORN HOLDER - £50987.47 in revenue
13. SPOTTY BUNTING - £42700.02 in revenue
14. JUMBO BAG PINK POLKADOT - £41619.66 in revenue
15. mailout - £40991.38 in revenue
16. BLACK RECORD COVER FRAME - £40596.96 in revenue
17. SET OF 3 CAKE TINS PANTRY DESIGN  - £37413.44 in revenue
18. DOORMAT KEEP CALM AND COME IN - £36565.39 in revenue
19. JAM MAKING SET WITH JARS - £36116.09 in revenue
20. WOOD BLACK BOARD ANT WHITE FINISH - £35859.27 in revenue
21. LUNCH BAG RED RETROSPOT - £35187.31 in revenue
22. HOT WATER BOTTLE TEA AND SYMPATHY - £32692.49 in revenue
23. VICTORIAN GLASS HANGING T-LIGHT - £32549.57 in revenue
24. CHOCOLATE HOT WATER BOTTLE - £32317.30 in revenue
25. JUMBO BAG STRAWBERRY - £32121.98 in revenue
```

Figure 5-20. Console log of my local tests to double-check the tools' calculations and reference figures for items sold and revenue generated

If I were to choose one of these tools, I'd select Julius. While its UX is very similar to ChatGPT's, and even the underlying model is in part the same (GPT-4, as I write this in mid-2024), its data analysis capabilities, such as rendering charts in the chat conversation, are not available in ChatGPT.

I rated all three tools between 5 and 7 (Table 5-1), given these shortcomings. I expect these tools to evolve a lot in the coming years, but in my opinion, they are not yet reliable enough that you can simply give them a large volume of data, ask questions, and trust the results. If you use them, I recommend running scripts locally to double-check the numbers. (It's OK if your scripts are generated by AI tools, since you can review and modify the code and have full visibility and control over the data analysis, as you saw in Chapters 2 and 3.)

Table 5-1. AI data analysis tools overview

Tool	UX	Test performance
Julius	Chatbot	7/10
Akkio	Chatbot	5/10
ChatGPT	Chatbot	6/10

Conclusion

After more than 15 years working with software development and data science teams, I can confidently say that AI tools have the potential to become game-changers in how we handle data analysis and business intelligence. Their ability to clean and analyze massive datasets in seconds, rather than days, will transform what's possible for businesses of all sizes.

Furthermore, from my experience working with a wide range of business stakeholders, from early-stage startup founders to business teams at Fortune 500 companies, I can easily imagine these AI tools empowering nontechnical stakeholders to extract insights from their data. The effects of that empowerment could be immense. In some cases, it might mean skipping costly data engineering projects; in other cases, it just makes those projects faster and less expensive.

With that, here's my word of caution: the tools are not there yet. While the results can be very impressive on the surface, they come with significant flaws, calculation errors, and generic explanations. A distracted user might be easily fooled by the instant reward of good-looking charts and insights, but overlooking such shortcomings can result in serious negative consequences. Business stakeholders could make decisions that reduce the value of their business; data analysts who delegate their work to these tools might end up performing poorly in their jobs.

These tools are already powerful and useful. But they have limitations, and the "black box" effect can make it very hard to identify those limitations. Always be specific in your prompts, and always double-check the results by doing manual analysis or running local scripts. I always tell my teams to treat AI-generated insights like advice from a colleague: while it's valuable input, always validate it and do your own critical thinking before making any big decisions.

CHAPTER 6

Documentation and Technical Writing

Documentation is vital for clarity, consistency, and knowledge transfer in software development. It ensures that team members understand the code when onboarding and reduces the learning curve during day-to-day work, leaving less room for lost context and the consequent errors and refactorings.

Documentation is also important for nontechnical stakeholders such as product managers, customer-support representatives, and those working in marketing, sales, and operations. Clear documentation fosters collaboration across teams and creates a single source of truth that prevents miscommunication. As software evolves, proper documentation simplifies codebase maintenance and onboarding for new developers, bolstering the longevity of the project.

Outside the company, documenting how to use a software product can help sales and marketing efforts, prevent difficulties during customer onboarding, and foster user engagement with the product. Writing features and workflows down for external stakeholders is also a great starting point for collecting their feedback on how to improve the product.

Despite its importance, documentation often doesn't get written at all. Software engineers don't usually enjoy writing for humans, so they often skip it if they can. But they are almost always under deadline pressure, and when they have to make compromises, documentation is often one of the things left behind. Even when it does get written, heavy workloads and time pressure often lead to rushed or incomplete content. Writing high-quality documentation takes time. Additional challenges include finding the right level of detail and keeping documentation up to date as systems evolve.

AI tools were helping generate written content for many years before the recent LLM-driven AI wave. Writing tools such as Grammarly, which helps find the correct words and fix mistakes, are especially helpful for those writing in a foreign language. In software development, tools such as Swagger and Javadoc also use AI to automatically generate API documentation in tandem with code updates.

The tools I review in this chapter were launched more recently, mostly since the generative AI wave started in 2022, and all aim to extend the simplicity of generating documentation from code beyond simple modules (like APIs) and helpers (like Grammarly). Some aim to be competent enough to replace the need for human action in writing documentation.

Types of Documentation

There are four key types of documentation commonly found in software development:

API/SDK documentation
: A critical resource for developers, documentation of APIs and software development kits (SDKs), provides clear, structured details about the functions, methods, and services available within a software system. These documentation interfaces serve as a bridge between different software components, ensuring that developers can integrate and use the system efficiently.

Internal documentation and feature specifications
: When business stakeholders define a new product or feature to be developed in order to fulfill a business objective, they write feature specifications to let software engineers know what functionalities to implement. The engineers' role is to extend those specifications with technical system designs, architectural decisions, and workflows that document not just *what* was implemented, but also *how* it was implemented. This type of documentation is vital for maintaining and evolving software projects over time, especially when the original engineers are no longer around.

User guides and manuals
: These documents help nontechnical users understand how to use the software. They include everything from installation instructions to troubleshooting tips. They're useful during the sales process as support material for sales and marketing colleagues, and as customers use the product. The challenge here lies in writing documentation for users who don't have a technical background.

Release notes and changelogs
: These documents are used to communicate changes to the software, such as bug fixes, new features, or performance improvements. More than just keeping everyone informed, effective release notes inform both internal and external stakeholders of the need to update integrations and workflows to accommodate the changes.

Evaluation Process

I evaluated more than 20 AI tools in the documentation and technical writing space in order to shortlist the four highlighted in this chapter. Every tool covered here meets the following criteria:

- It is a professional project with a competent team behind it.
- It generates high-quality results.
- It offers some level of functionality for free or on a trial basis.
- It has a high level of adoption at the time of writing (mid-2025).

For this test, I created a very simple authentication flow, with both frontend and backend. The full code, which is available in this book's GitHub repository (*https://github.com/sergiopereira-io/oreilly_book*), contains flows for signup, login, and logout. I've used the AI tools in this chapter to document my code. My main point of comparison is whether the documentation produced can be useful for any of the four documentation use cases explained previously.

Again, for this test I gave preference to tools that can be used with a simple signup and free trial, so I stayed away from enterprise tools.

The full documentation generated for each test can be found in the book's GitHub repository (*https://github.com/sergiopereira-io/oreilly_book*).

Swimm

Swimm (*https://swimm.io*) is an AI-powered documentation tool designed specifically for software engineers. It automates the creation and maintenance of code documentation. To ensure that it stays current with every code change, Swimm integrates directly into the code repository. Engineers can create documentation for a certain code file or snippet, or create/update documentation with each new pull request (PR). The latter option is a great fit for most software development teams' processes, since a PR represents the most granular level of iteration to the codebase. Each such iteration needs to be documented, and each has the potential to render the existing documentation outdated.

I think this flow is comparable to the automated code reviews in Chapter 3. I can see how embedding these tools into a repo can provide a seamless integration into existing software development processes.

While Swimm can be blended into the repo and create or update documentation upon each PR, for the sake of this comparison test, I haven't used that exact flow. I've simply used Swimm's browser-based UI, which allows me to connect the repo, select specific files to be documented, and prompt for what to include in the documentation, as shown in Figure 6-1.

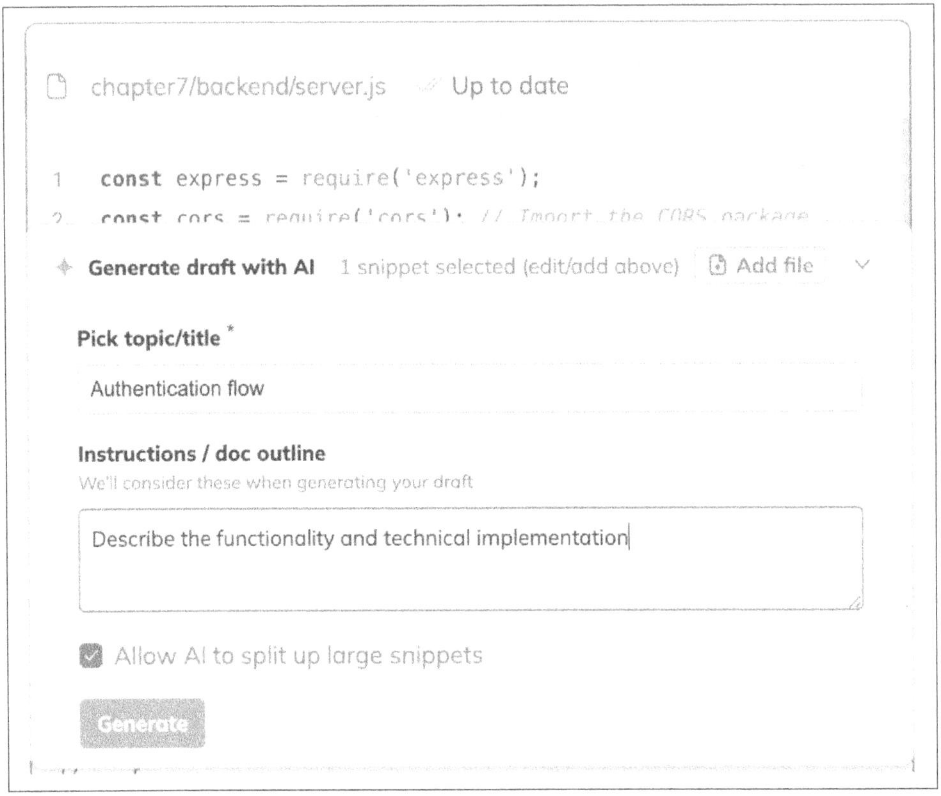

Figure 6-1. Swimm's widget to create a piece of documentation

In this flow, I've asked Swimm to document the backend part of my authentication flow with a simple prompt:

```
Describe the functionality and technical implementation.
```

The desired output is a document that can be used for internal visibility on ongoing initiatives and for onboarding future team members. You can see a sample of the result in Figure 6-2.

The authentication routes are then integrated with the server, allowing us to handle authentication-related requests:

```
chapter7/backend/server.js        Up to date

20   // Create users table if it doesn't exist
21   db.run('CREATE TABLE IF NOT EXISTS users (id INTEGER PRIMARY KEY AUTOINCREMENT,
22
23   // Use the routes for authentication
24   app.use('/api/auth', authRoutes(db));
25
26   // Start the server
27   app.listen(port, () => {
28     console.log(`Server running at http://localhost:${port}`);
29   });
```

```
chapter7/frontend/index.html      Up to date

1    <!DOCTYPE html>
2    <html lang="en">
```

Generate draft with AI 1 snippet selected (edit/add above) Add file ⌄

Pick topic/title *

Frontend test plan

Instructions / doc outline
We'll consider these when generating your draft

Describe the frontend flows and create a test plan for each flow.

☑ Allow AI to split up large snippets

Generate

Figure 6-2. Sample of Swimm's output for the backend documentation

This output is quite good. I like the structure of the document as well as its content. However, my authentication flow is probably too simple to showcase Swimm's full potential. So I tested a second example for a more complex document:

```
Describe the frontend code and create a test plan for each flow.
```

The result was again very good. It generated a full document (whose table of contents can be found in Figure 6-3), including a high-level introduction and then a deep dive into specific code components that impact the flow and thus should be documented.

Figure 6-3. Table of contents of the document generated by Swimm for the frontend code

The last section of the document, as I asked, identifies the main flows of my code and provides test plans for each. The actual test plans are quite simplistic, but that's probably a byproduct of the simplicity of the underlying flow, as shown here:

Test plan

Test login flow

1. Verify the login form is visible by default.
2. Enter valid credentials and submit; expect a success message.
3. Enter invalid credentials and submit; expect an error alert.
4. Click "Register here" and ensure the registration form appears.

Test registration flow

1. Click "Register here" to switch to the registration form.
2. Enter valid details and submit; expect a success message.
3. Enter invalid details and submit; expect an error alert.
4. Click "Login here" and ensure the login form reappears.

Test success and logout

1. After successful login or registration, verify the success message is displayed.
2. Click the logout button and ensure the login form is shown again.

Swimm did well in this test. It was easy to get started with this tool, and it generated relevant documentation for my requests in correct Markdown format, which is the standard in technical documentation. However, I found it quite limiting that Swimm can only document one file of code at a time. This produces very fragmented pieces of documentation that are closer to a *read.me* file than a higher-level codebase and flow documentation.

I see working with a larger scope of source material as a natural evolution for Swimm, which could leverage its superior integration flow to create documentation for the whole codebase, or at least groups of files. It could work horizontally, documenting the structure of frontend code by using all frontend files as the object of a document, or vertically, documenting a feature flow by using all files related to that feature.

As such, I'm rating Swimm a 6/10. While the UX is good, the output is still far from the quality of documentation that I would accept from my teams.

ChatGPT

ChatGPT (*https://chat.openai.com*) is most software engineers' go-to LLM tool for creating documentation, so I'm including it in this chapter, specifically the GPT-4o model, the most advanced available at the time of writing (mid-2025).

I started by prompting ChatGPT to generate the documentation for my code. I included in the prompt all six code files, a screenshot of the repository structure (so it understands the relationships between the code files), and instructions for what the documentation should include, as seen in Figure 6-4.

> Generate documentation for the code base attached, which
> contains:
> - An image with the repository structure
> - The files from the repository
>
> The documentation aims to be used in a software develpoment team, by both technical and non-technical stakeholders. This documentation must include functional descriptions of the workflows, as well as technical descriptions of the implementation.

Figure 6-4. Instructions to ChatGPT to document my code

ChatGPT generated very comprehensive documentation, as seen in the table of contents in Figure 6-5.

Table of Contents

1. Overview
2. Repository Structure
    - Backend
    - Frontend
3. Functional Workflow
    - 1. User Registration
    - 2. User Login
    - 3. Frontend Behavior
4. Technical Implementation
    - Backend
    - Frontend
5. APIs
    - Register User
    - Login User
6. Future Improvements
7. How to Run Locally
8. Conclusion

Figure 6-5. Table of contents of the documentation generated by ChatGPT

This is a really good output; it's very complete documentation with sections for all of the expected main components, from high-level context (such as repository structure) to a detailed deep dive in each specific component, such as the API, visible in Figure 6-6.

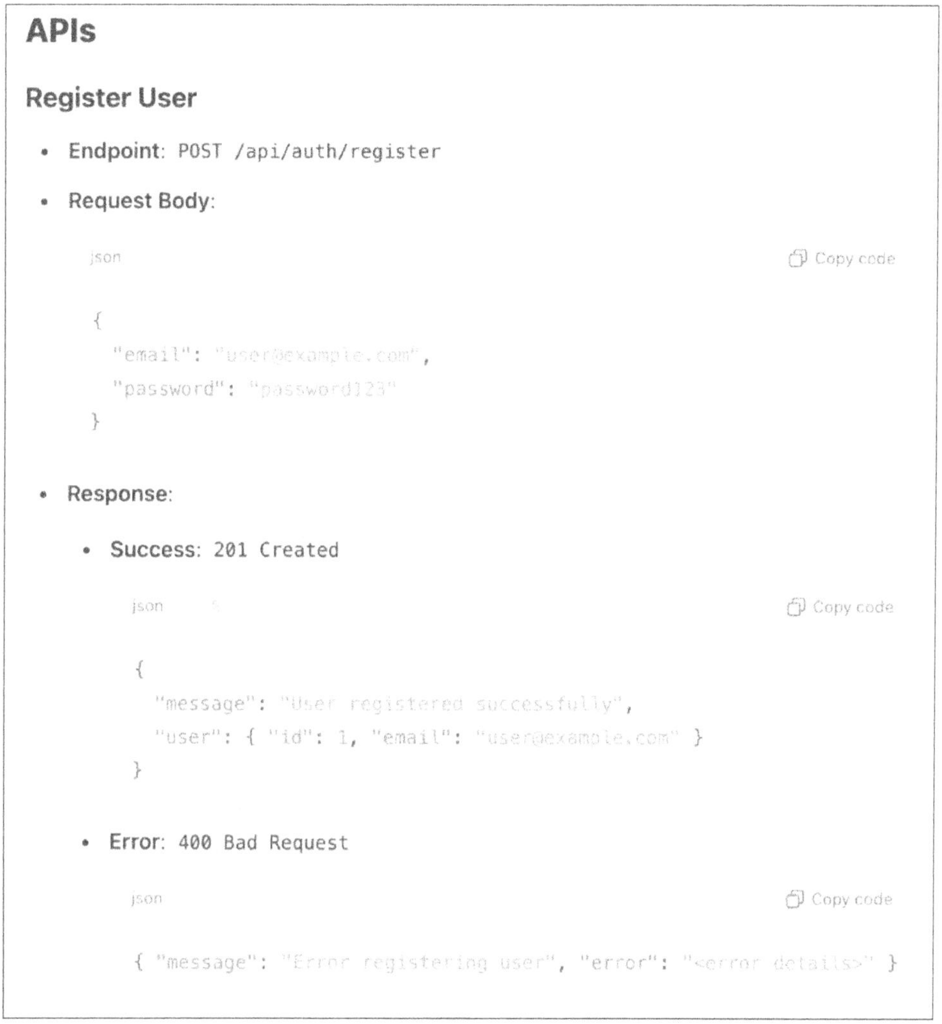

APIs

Register User

- **Endpoint**: `POST /api/auth/register`
- **Request Body**:

```json
{
  "email": "user@example.com",
  "password": "password123"
}
```

- **Response**:
  - **Success**: `201 Created`

```json
{
  "message": "User registered successfully",
  "user": { "id": 1, "email": "user@example.com" }
}
```

  - **Error**: `400 Bad Request`

```json
{ "message": "Error registering user", "error": "<error details>" }
```

Figure 6-6. ChatGPT's documentation of the API module

You can ask ChatGPT to output the documentation directly into a Markdown file. I committed the final documentation generated by ChatGPT (as well as the other tools in this chapter) to the book's GitHub repository (*https://github.com/sergiopereira-io/oreilly_book*).

As expected, ChatGPT performs very well in this limited-scope test. It will work with up to 20 files at a time, and the file size limit varies by file type. While that's totally OK for small projects like my authentication application, it is insufficient for most production-level applications. On top of those limits, ChatGPT also offers an inconvenient UI, compared to tools that connect to the repository. The need to upload files manually and give ChatGPT contextual information about their structure and relationships makes it more challenging to use, especially for large projects.

As such, I'm rating ChatGPT a 7/10 for this use case. The quality of the documentation is very good, with the caveat of the limits and inconvenient UI. It would take a software engineer some creativity to document clusters of an application (by functionality or part of the stack, or module) within the limit of 20 files per piece of documentation.

Cursor

Cursor (*https://www.cursor.com*) is a relatively new player in the AI coding tool space. It was launched in 2023 and has captured massive market share in the specific category of IDEs with AI code-assistant capabilities, which has been led by GitHub Copilot. As of August 2024, Cursor had 40,000 customers.[1]

Cursor's product is an AI-native IDE that started as a fork from the popular Visual Studio Code. It allows software engineers to select which LLM should power the tool; I've used Anthropic's Claude 3.5 Sonnet. As an actual IDE, Cursor has visibility into all code files in my repository, regardless of their number or size. You enter prompts through a chat feature, as shown in Figure 6-7.

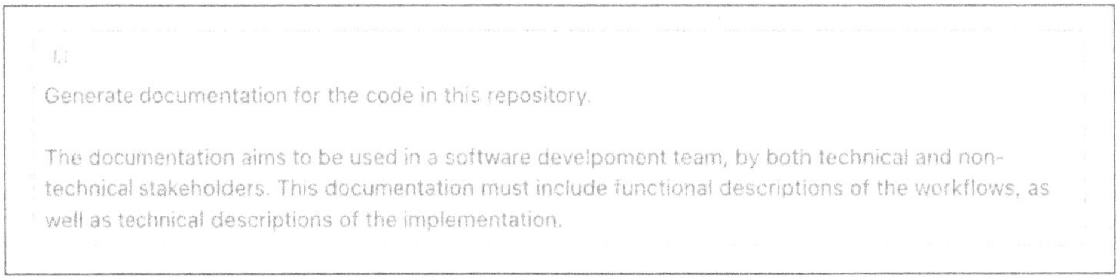

Generate documentation for the code in this repository.
The documentation aims to be used in a software develpoment team, by both technical and non-technical stakeholders. This documentation must include functional descriptions of the workflows, as well as technical descriptions of the implementation.

Figure 6-7. Prompt to Cursor to generate documentation

1 Anysphere Team. August 22, 2024. "Series A and Magic" (*https://www.cursor.com/blog/series-a*). *Cursor* (blog).

The document Cursor generated was good, with sections for the expected main components, as seen in the table of contents in Figure 6-8.

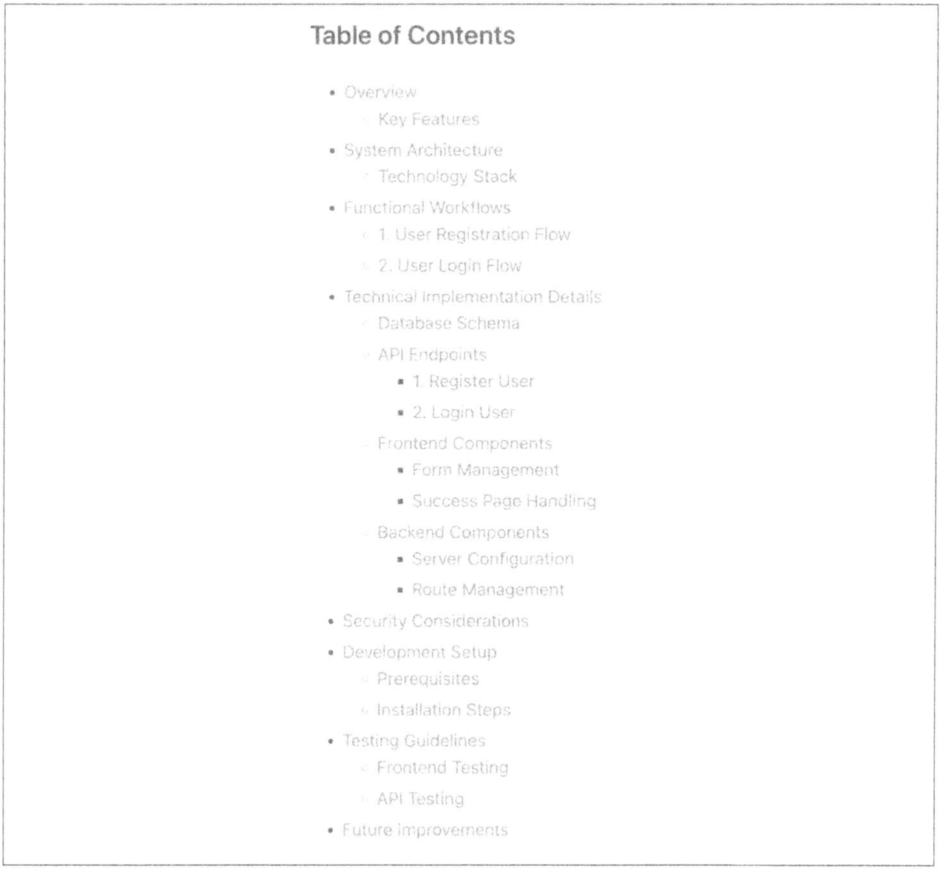

Table of Contents

- Overview
  - Key Features
- System Architecture
  - Technology Stack
- Functional Workflows
  - 1. User Registration Flow
  - 2. User Login Flow
- Technical Implementation Details
  - Database Schema
  - API Endpoints
    - 1. Register User
    - 2. Login User
  - Frontend Components
    - Form Management
    - Success Page Handling
  - Backend Components
    - Server Configuration
    - Route Management
- Security Considerations
- Development Setup
  - Prerequisites
  - Installation Steps
- Testing Guidelines
  - Frontend Testing
  - API Testing
- Future Improvements

Figure 6-8. Table of contents of the documentation generated by Cursor

Despite the very comprehensive outline and the relevancy of its content, Cursor has a significant pitfall when it comes to generating Markdown documents. For some reason (perhaps a bug), the generated content is only partially formatted as a Markdown file. It outputs some sections as raw text, such as the snippet in Figure 6-9. This makes it much harder to read.

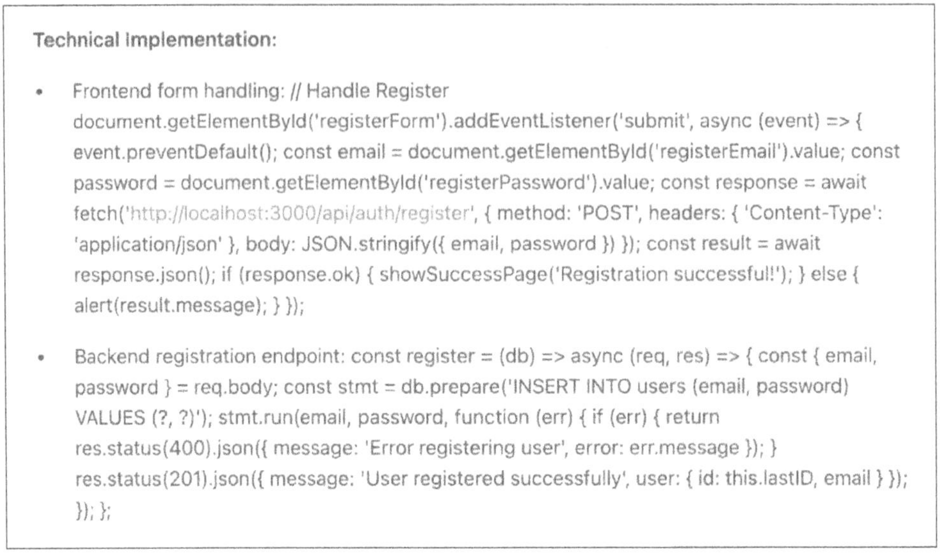
Technical Implementation:

- Frontend form handling: // Handle Register document.getElementById('registerForm').addEventListener('submit', async (event) => { event.preventDefault(); const email = document.getElementById('registerEmail').value; const password = document.getElementById('registerPassword').value; const response = await fetch('http://localhost:3000/api/auth/register', { method: 'POST', headers: { 'Content-Type': 'application/json' }, body: JSON.stringify({ email, password }) }); const result = await response.json(); if (response.ok) { showSuccessPage('Registration successful!'); } else { alert(result.message); } });
- Backend registration endpoint: const register = (db) => async (req, res) => { const { email, password } = req.body; const stmt = db.prepare('INSERT INTO users (email, password) VALUES (?, ?)'); stmt.run(email, password, function (err) { if (err) { return res.status(400).json({ message: 'Error registering user', error: err.message }); } res.status(201).json({ message: 'User registered successfully', user: { id: this.lastID, email } }); }); };

Figure 6-9. Formatting issue in Cursor's generated Markdown document

Despite these formatting issues, the documentation generated is extensive, covers the right topics, and has the correct level of technical depth. It's definitely in line with what I would consider acceptable documentation from my teams. As such, I rate Cursor 8/10.

Scribe

Scribe (*https://scribehow.com*) is a very different tool from the others reviewed in this chapter. This tool is best suited for creating user guides, standard operating procedures (SOPs), or bug reports in a visual way. While my use of Swimm, ChatGPT, and Cursor focused on creating written documentation about the technical implementation of a certain product or functionality, I used Scribe to produce a guide about the product's functionality.

While Scribe was created in 2019 as a basic screen capture tool, the functionality I used for this test, called Scribe AI, was only launched in 2023. It leverages the original functionality that allows a user to record a browser session, but instead of simply storing the video of the recording, it also creates an entire workflow with annotations, based on the screen transitions in the recording. That's why it caters to UI-related use cases, like bug reports and product guides.

To start the test, I installed Scribe's Chrome extension and used it to record a simple session of registering a new account and logging in to that account. My goal was for Scribe to generate a user guide that I could share with external nontechnical stakeholders, like users of the product.

The experience of recording my first session was quite seamless; I got the recording I needed easily on my first try. It's called a Scribe, the name for both the video recording and the annotated workflow that's generated, and it's available in this public link (*https://oreil.ly/lsVD3*). I'd say this output is good, since it identifies the screen transitions in my workflow and captures the screenshots of each screen, highlighting the action that the user did on the screen to cause the transition. The result is in line with user shadowing tools like Hotjar or Fullstory, which are commonly used for user research and bug tracking.

Scribe offers a feature that converts the raw HTML document in the preceding public link into an AI-generated document. I used the authentication flow to test the feature, which allows the user to write a prompt specifying the documentation piece to be generated from the screen recording. My instructions were simple, as shown in Figure 6-10.

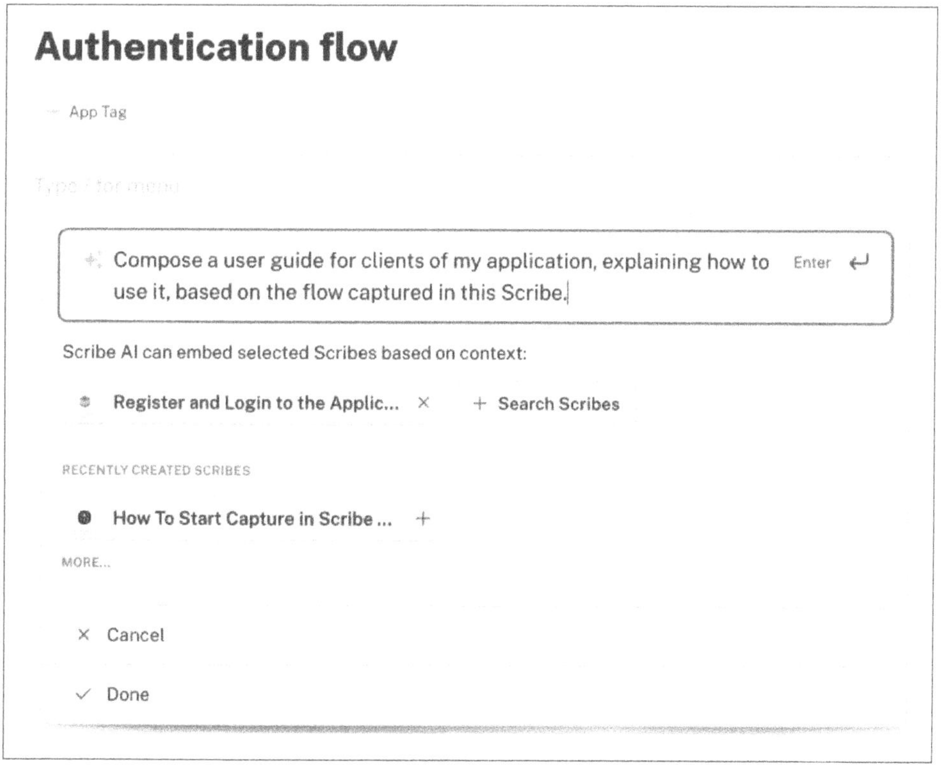

Figure 6-10. Instructions to Scribe to generate a document from raw tracking of website actions

The resulting document is publicly available here (*https://oreil.ly/WcT6u*). I found this output underwhelming. It's generic; it feels like it could have been written about any application, not specifically about mine. It generated a document and embedded

Scribes (specific flows) into it, as opposed to generating a document based on the flow I recorded, which was my intention. This makes me think that the tool might be a better fit to generate larger pieces of documentation that involve several different Scribes merged together in a large document (e.g., a product guide). The content of the generated document is not very relevant to the use case. As such, I'm rating Scribe a 5/10.

Tool Comparison

Table 6-1 compares the ratings for each of the tools discussed in the chapter.

Table 6-1. AI documentation tools overview

Tool	UX	Test performance
Swimm	Repository extension	6/10
ChatGPT	Website	7/10
Cursor	IDE	8/10
Scribe	Chrome extension	5/10

Conclusion

As a CTO for over a decade, I've found that documentation is one of those things that's always lacking, but never to the point where it's worth pausing ongoing work to fix it. In fact, bad documentation is a form of technical debt, but one that doesn't break systems or degrade performance. It *does* degrade the *team's* performance, however, which is a less visible and perhaps more damaging form of debt in a software development team.

I've always found it hard to push software engineers in my teams to write documentation in the first place, and even harder to keep that documentation organized, accessible, and updated. I think that AI tools like the ones I reviewed in this chapter can play a fundamental role in making that process easier. With a simple prompt, they can generate documentation within seconds. It would take a human at least an hour or two to generate a similar document. And that time commitment compounds with complexity: the larger a system is, the more challenging and time-consuming it is to document it properly and keep that documentation up to date. In a team of a few dozen people, that work could easily add up to thousands of collective hours of work a year.

While AI tools can create documentation instantly, they can also create bad documentation (just like humans can). I recommend that teams take the same approach to documentation as to setting coding guidelines: create a template for prompts or even for documents, with predefined sections and subsections. This serves as a backstop to avoid unnecessarily long documents, and facilitates readability by making content easier to find.

With all that said, documentation created by AI tools must *always* be thoroughly reviewed and edited by team members. While it takes seconds to produce 90% of the deliverable, the final revisions and quality control must be performed by human beings, since the output does not always fulfill the objective. See the case with Scribe, where the document generated is generic; a human reviewer would have caught that flaw and improved the documentation manually.

CHAPTER 7
Chatbots and Virtual Assistants

Chatbots have been a staple of digital customer service and automation for over a decade. Initially built as simple rule-based programs, traditional chatbots followed predefined logic trees to handle repetitive tasks, such as answering frequently asked questions, providing automated responses in customer support, or collecting user information in structured workflows. These chatbots weren't very powerful compared to today's LLM-based bots, but they became a very popular way to automate high-volume, low-complexity interactions. However, their technical implementations struggled with unstructured conversations, ambiguity, or user inputs that deviated from expected patterns. The experience usually felt rigid and unnatural—people clearly understood they were talking to a machine, and those user interactions would frequently end with frustrating statements like, "I don't understand. Please try again."

Now that people are used to chatting with LLM-based tools like ChatGPT, the rule-based approach to chatbots seems like a distant memory. Today's AI-powered chatbots no longer rely solely on predefined scripts and rules. Instead, they leverage sophisticated natural language processing (NLP), contextual understanding, and generative AI to deliver dynamic, humanlike interactions. These advancements mean the role of chatbots has significantly expanded to include tasks like:

- Understanding complex queries and responding with relevant, well-formed answers
- Maintaining memory across conversations, providing continuity and context
- Taking actions on behalf of users, such as booking appointments or retrieving personalized data
- Learning and adapting over time, improving based on real-world interactions
- Integrating with external APIs and databases to fetch real-time information

This transformation means that software engineers now have a broad spectrum of tools and frameworks available to help us build intelligent chatbots, ranging from no-code workflow builders to fully customizable AI-powered assistants that leverage agentic reasoning and training data. Whether you want to build a simple automated helpdesk bot or a sophisticated AI agent capable of complex decision-making, the technology is now more accessible than ever.

Types of Chatbot Implementations

There are three main options for implementing a chatbot:

No-code AI chatbots
: These tools promise that users without any programming knowledge will be able to deploy AI-powered assistants. They usually have easy-to-use interfaces where users can upload datasets, define workflows, and select the underlying AI models. While these tools are promoted for a nontechnical audience, I'm including them in the book because, in my experience, certain technical knowledge is often required to integrate these tools with other parts of a company's workflow, and this ends up being part of software engineers' scope of work.

  These no-code chatbots are a natural evolution of the rule-based chatbots mentioned previously and cater to the same use cases: customer support, ecommerce, and FAQ automation.

Drag-and-drop chatbot builders
: These tools aim to bridge the gap between simplicity and flexibility to adapt to the needs of different clients. They are usually easy to set up and allow users to build conversation flows visually by connecting boxes with predefined functionalities, while integrating AI-powered features for dynamic interactions. Developers can automate workflows and use more complex logic in the backend for the chatbot.

  These chatbot builders cater to use cases such as customer service, lead generation, and internal workflow automation.

Code-based AI frameworks
: These are usually SDKs, APIs, or open source repositories that allow software engineers to fully control the chatbot's behavior, which they'll then use as boilerplate to implement customized chatbot experiences. They tend to have higher standards for training data. Use cases include agentic reasoning, integration with other tools and workflows, and even data security (since these chatbots can be self-hosted on a company's cloud infrastructure).

Evaluation Process

To compare chatbot-building tools, I created a chatbot that interacts with this Online Retail Dataset (*https://github.com/sergiopereira-io/oreilly_book/blob/main/chapter8/data/product-catalog.csv*), created by Lucas Soares, a fellow O'Reilly author in the field of machine learning. It consists of transactional data from an ecommerce shop; I've used it to test chatbots' capabilities to retrieve factual data and answer complex user queries.

Each chatbot was tested using a set of predefined queries, evaluating its:

- Ease of setup and deployment
- Ability to retrieve factual information
- Context retention across multiple interactions
- Ability to handle complex queries

I tested multiple tools, but I have included one from each of the categories outlined in the previous section.

Let's begin with a no-code option: Chatbase.

Chatbase

Chatbase (*https://www.chatbase.co*) was launched in 2022 as a no-code AI chatbot builder that allows users to create and train chatbots by uploading documents or datasets. It gained popularity due to its simple interface and integration with OpenAI's GPT models, which made it an accessible solution for businesses looking to automate their support and customer interactions without the need for technical expertise. While the product is still relatively young, Chatbase has seen adoption among small businesses, solopreneurs, and startups, particularly for handling customer support and FAQ automation. The tool offers a free-tier option and a paid plan for scaling your chatbot's capabilities.

For this test, I created a free account on the Chatbase website and looked for a way to create my chatbot. I quickly found the place to add the training data, my spreadsheet with the ecommerce product catalog (see Figure 7-1). In a matter of two or three minutes, I was interacting with my chatbot.

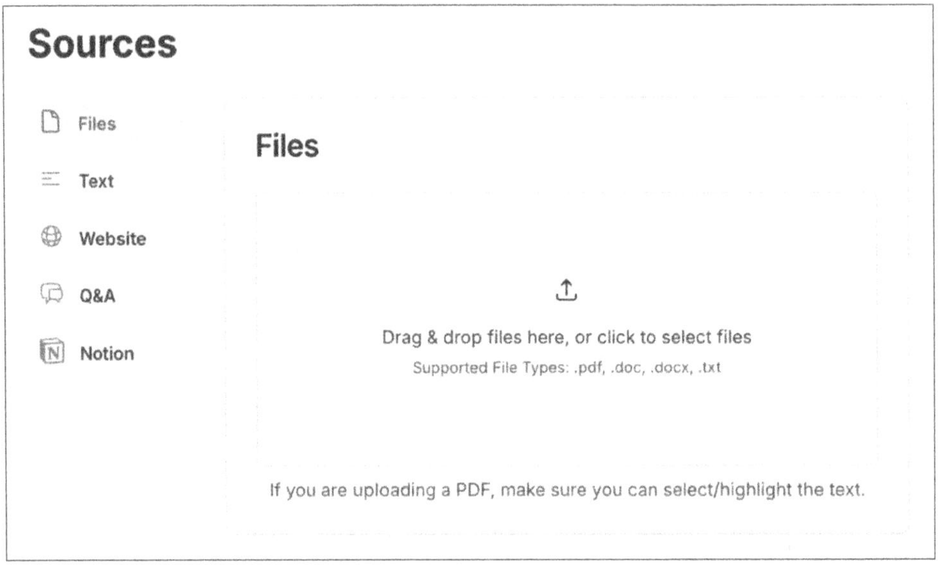

Figure 7-1. Chatbase's Sources UI, where users can add training data

Once the chatbot was ready, I started asking questions, as if I were a real client:

```
I see there are some Android phones in your catalog. Compare the
features and prices, and tell me the best budget Android phones.
```

It did well with the first question, fetching correct results and displaying them in a well-formatted response, as shown in Figure 7-2.

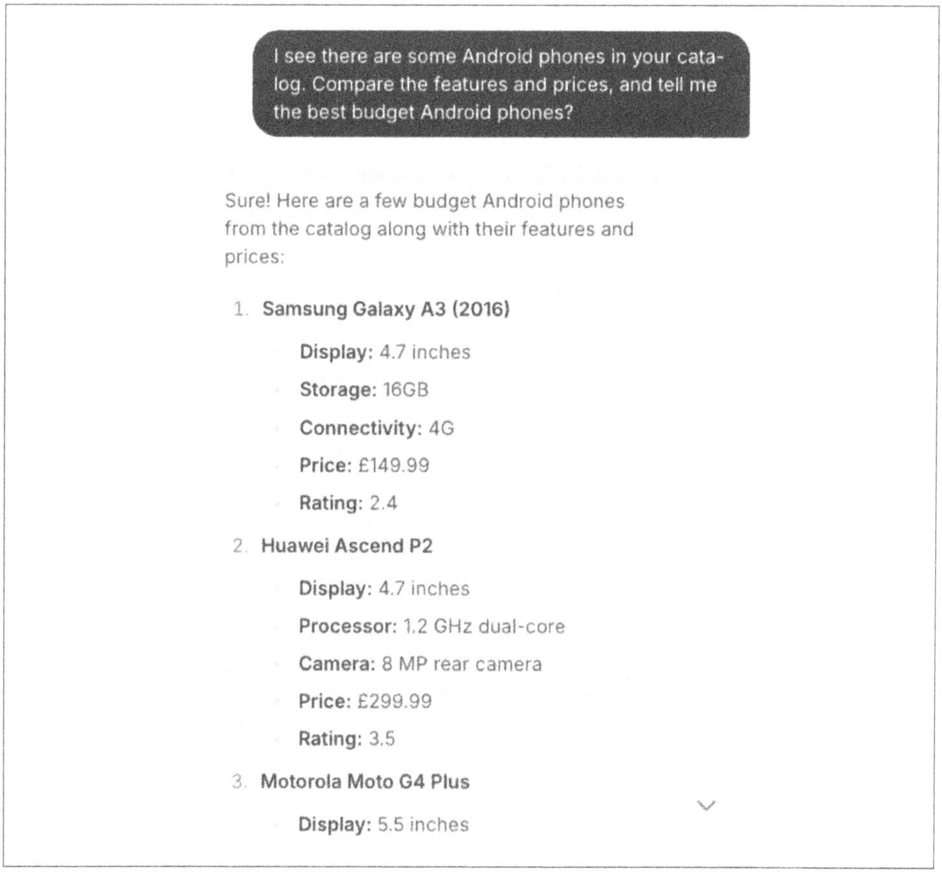

Figure 7-2. First question to my Chatbase chatbot (truncated to the visible area)

In the second question, I purposely asked about a product that doesn't exist:

```
I'm looking for a laptop below $10. What's the best option?
```

This is a common source of hallucinations, and once again, my Chatbase bot did well, stating that no product matches my query (see Figure 7-3).

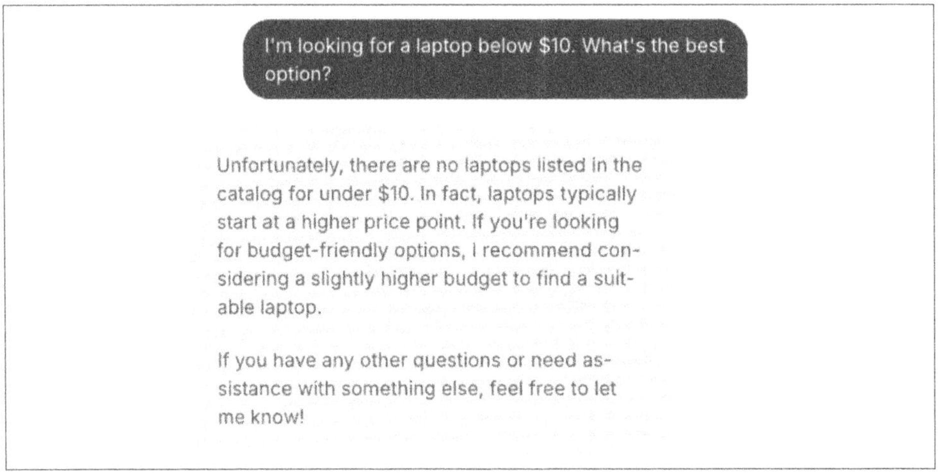

I'm looking for a laptop below $10. What's the best option?
Unfortunately, there are no laptops listed in the catalog for under $10. In fact, laptops typically start at a higher price point. If you're looking for budget-friendly options, I recommend considering a slightly higher budget to find a suitable laptop.
If you have any other questions or need assistance with something else, feel free to let me know!

Figure 7-3. Second question to my Chatbase chatbot

For the third question, I asked something more complex, not only inquiring about specific products in the catalog, but also asking Chatbase to compare their attributes and ultimately provide a recommendation:

```
You have mobile phones and digital cameras. I'm interested in
photography, should I buy the Sony Xperia XA2 Ultra or the Pentax
K-1 camera? Why?
```

Again, my Chatbase bot did well, stating the attributes of each option and making recommendations about when to buy one or the other (see Figure 7-4).

Chatbase also makes it very easy to publish a chatbot using its Connect section. With a couple of clicks, I get some code to embed my chatbot in a website via a chat bubble or iframe. I was impressed by how easy it was to upload training data, test the bot, and publish it.

Chatbase did very well in the test, and it's probably one of the easiest ways to integrate a chatbot into a website, if you have specific training data and make some changes to the prompt to get the desired functionality, tone, and so on. As such, I rate it a 9/10. I didn't rate it 10/10 because the end product's behavior significantly resembles the default behavior of the underlying LLM (gpt-4o-mini, in this test). In other words, if a user were to upload the same training data to ChatGPT and ask these questions, the answers would be very similar. Still, the ease of doing all this and publishing the bot with a few clicks is impressive.

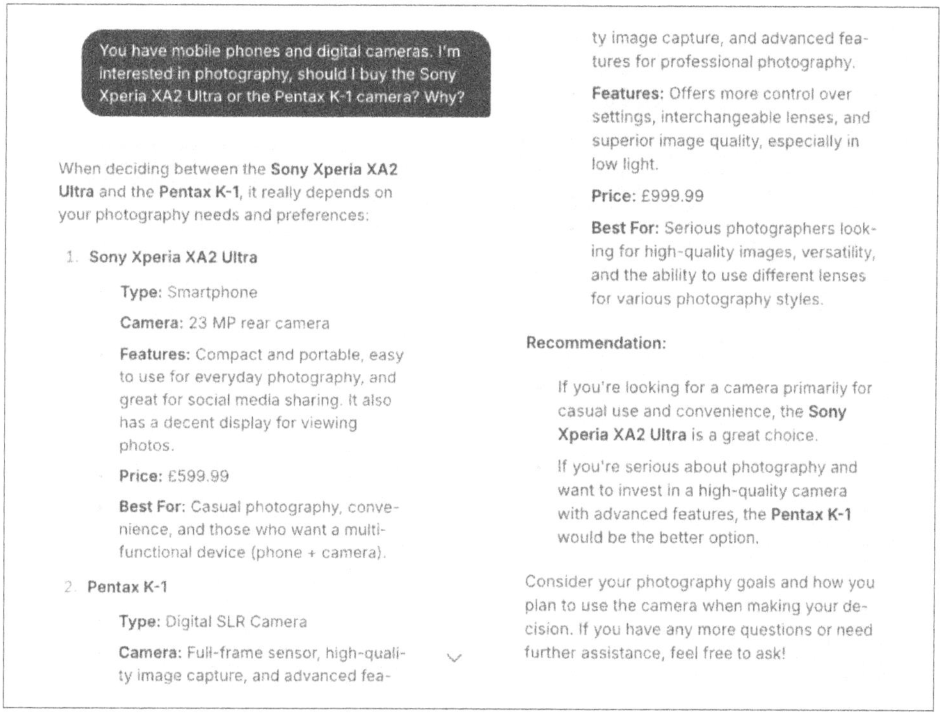

You have mobile phones and digital cameras. I'm interested in photography, should I buy the Sony Xperia XA2 Ultra or the Pentax K-1 camera? Why?
When deciding between the Sony Xperia XA2 Ultra and the Pentax K-1, it really depends on your photography needs and preferences:
1. Sony Xperia XA2 Ultra
Type: Smartphone
Camera: 23 MP rear camera
Features: Compact and portable, easy to use for everyday photography, and great for social media sharing. It also has a decent display for viewing photos.
Price: £599.99
Best For: Casual photography, convenience, and those who want a multi-functional device (phone + camera).
2. Pentax K-1
Type: Digital SLR Camera
Camera: Full-frame sensor, high-quality image capture, and advanced fea-
ty image capture, and advanced features for professional photography.
Features: Offers more control over settings, interchangeable lenses, and superior image quality, especially in low light.
Price: £999.99
Best For: Serious photographers looking for high-quality images, versatility, and the ability to use different lenses for various photography styles.
Recommendation:
If you're looking for a camera primarily for casual use and convenience, the Sony Xperia XA2 Ultra is a great choice.
If you're serious about photography and want to invest in a high-quality camera with advanced features, the Pentax K-1 would be the better option.
Consider your photography goals and how you plan to use the camera when making your decision. If you have any more questions or need further assistance, feel free to ask!

Figure 7-4. Third question to my Chatbase chatbot

Botpress

Drag-and-drop option Botpress (*https://botpress.com*) was founded as an open source chatbot-development platform back in 2017, when that meant rule-based chatbots. The current version of the product offers a visual builder that enables users to create complex conversational logic and to integrate the resulting bot with third-party APIs and other applications. In recent years, Botpress's adoption has grown, especially among midsize enterprises and organizations looking for an alternative to closed source chatbot platforms. With a modular architecture and self-hosting options, it appeals to businesses that need to comply with data privacy regulations while maintaining scalability.

To test Botpress, I followed the same playbook I used for Chatbase. I created a free account on the Botpress website and went through its widget to build an agent (that's what it calls a chatbot). It took me some time to figure out how to add the training data, since I first needed to create a table (its name for training data in CSV format) on a separate page, then add that as a knowledge base to my bot (see Figure 7-5).

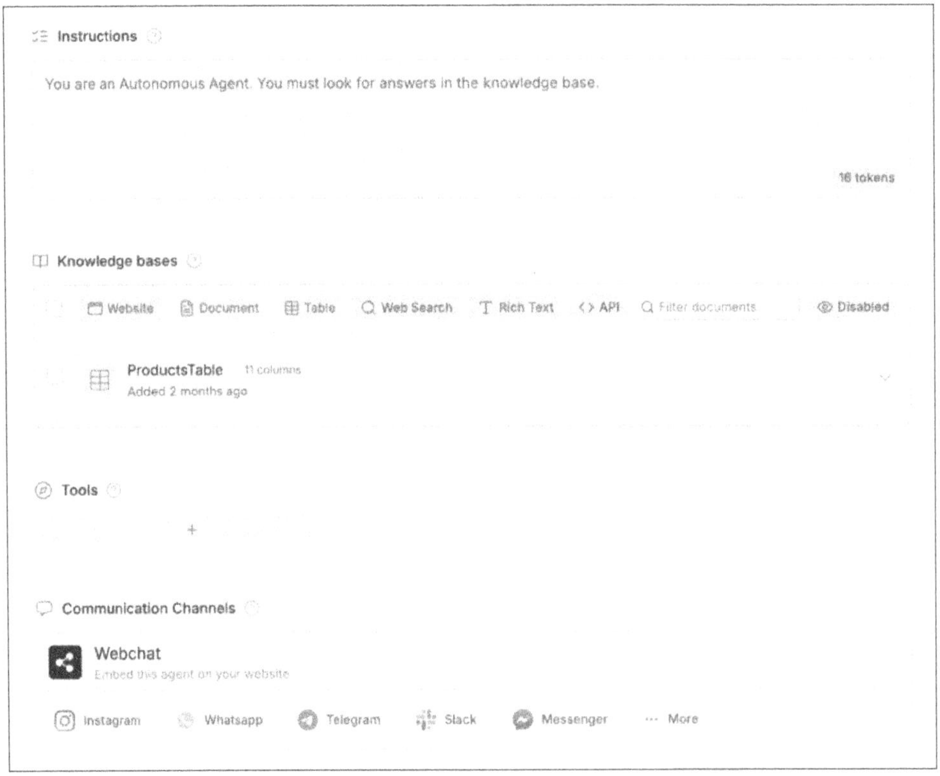

Figure 7-5. Botpress's Agent Builder UI, where users can add training data and configure their workflow

Botpress offers more options beyond a simple chatbot feature. Users can add different agents and tools and compose a workflow with them that serves as the backend reasoning under the bot's hood (see Figure 7-6). It's more powerful than Chatbase; however, getting a simple bot up and running took me 30 to 40 minutes of trial and error.

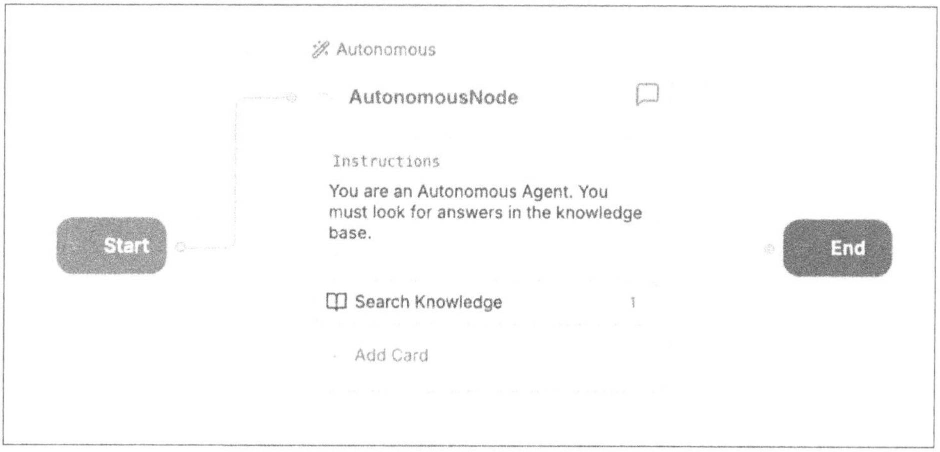

Figure 7-6. Botpress's workflow builder—I selected a very simple flow for my test

With the chatbot finally ready, I started interacting with it, asking the exact same questions I asked the Chatbase bot (see Figure 7-7).

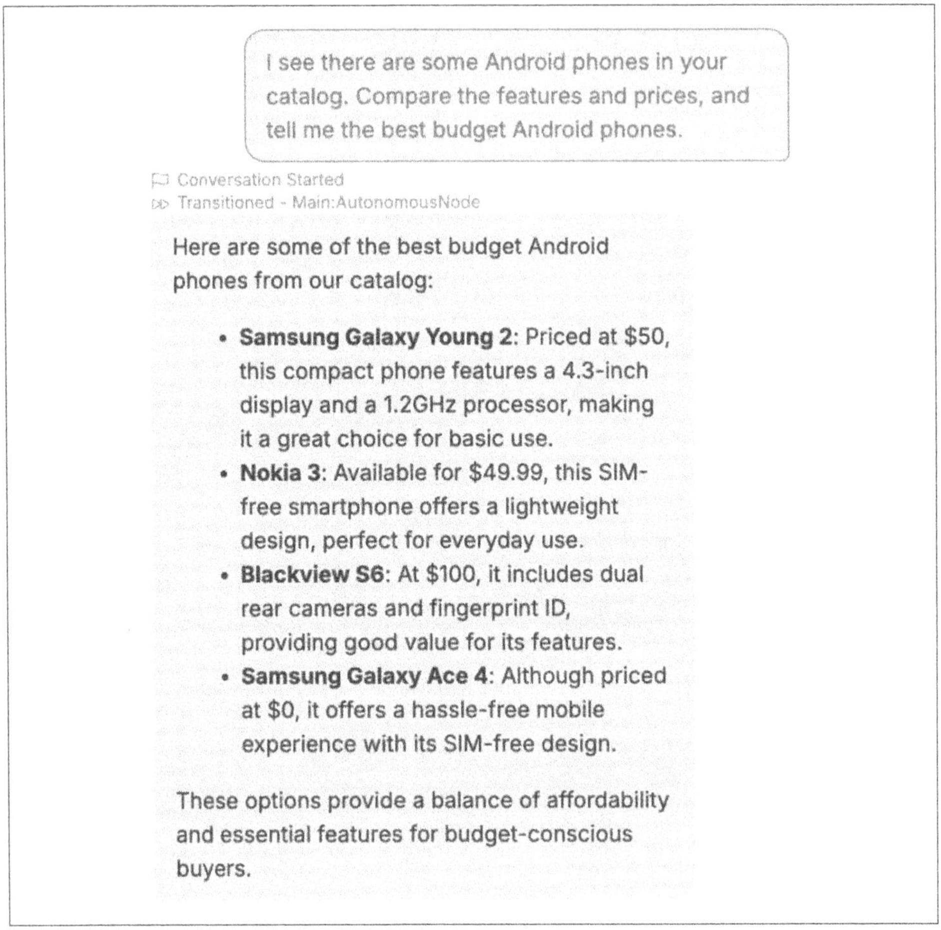

I see there are some Android phones in your catalog. Compare the features and prices, and tell me the best budget Android phones.
Conversation Started
Transitioned - Main:AutonomousNode
Here are some of the best budget Android phones from our catalog:
Samsung Galaxy Young 2: Priced at $50, this compact phone features a 4.3-inch display and a 1.2GHz processor, making it a great choice for basic use.
Nokia 3: Available for $49.99, this SIM-free smartphone offers a lightweight design, perfect for everyday use.
Blackview S6: At $100, it includes dual rear cameras and fingerprint ID, providing good value for its features.
Samsung Galaxy Ace 4: Although priced at $0, it offers a hassle-free mobile experience with its SIM-free design.
These options provide a balance of affordability and essential features for budget-conscious buyers.

Figure 7-7. First question to my Botpress chatbot

For the first question, the bot correctly fetched three budget Android phones; however, it also offered an option priced at $0, which is clearly a data error that it didn't flag to me. I'd be a bit frustrated with this suggestion if I were a real client.

Again, in the second question I purposefully asked about a product that doesn't exist, and my Botpress bot did well, correctly stating that no product matched my query (see Figure 7-8).

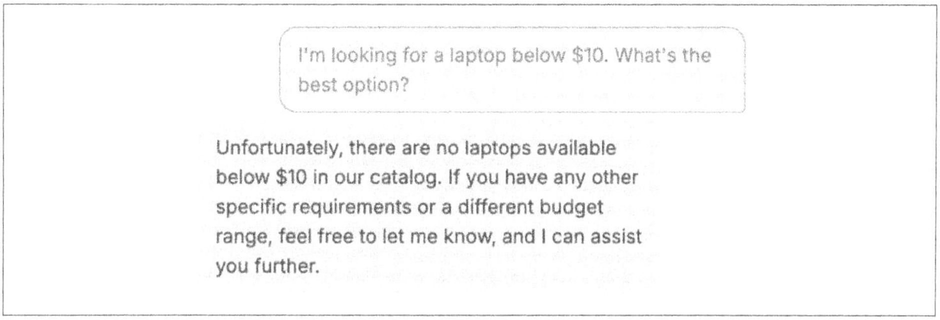

I'm looking for a laptop below $10. What's the best option?
Unfortunately, there are no laptops available below $10 in our catalog. If you have any other specific requirements or a different budget range, feel free to let me know, and I can assist you further.

Figure 7-8. Second question to my Botpress chatbot

Third, I once again asked a complex question about comparing the phone with the camera. My Botpress bot did well, stating the attributes of each option and when it recommended buying one or the other. The format wasn't great, however, since each product's attributes were packed into a single bullet point (see Figure 7-9).

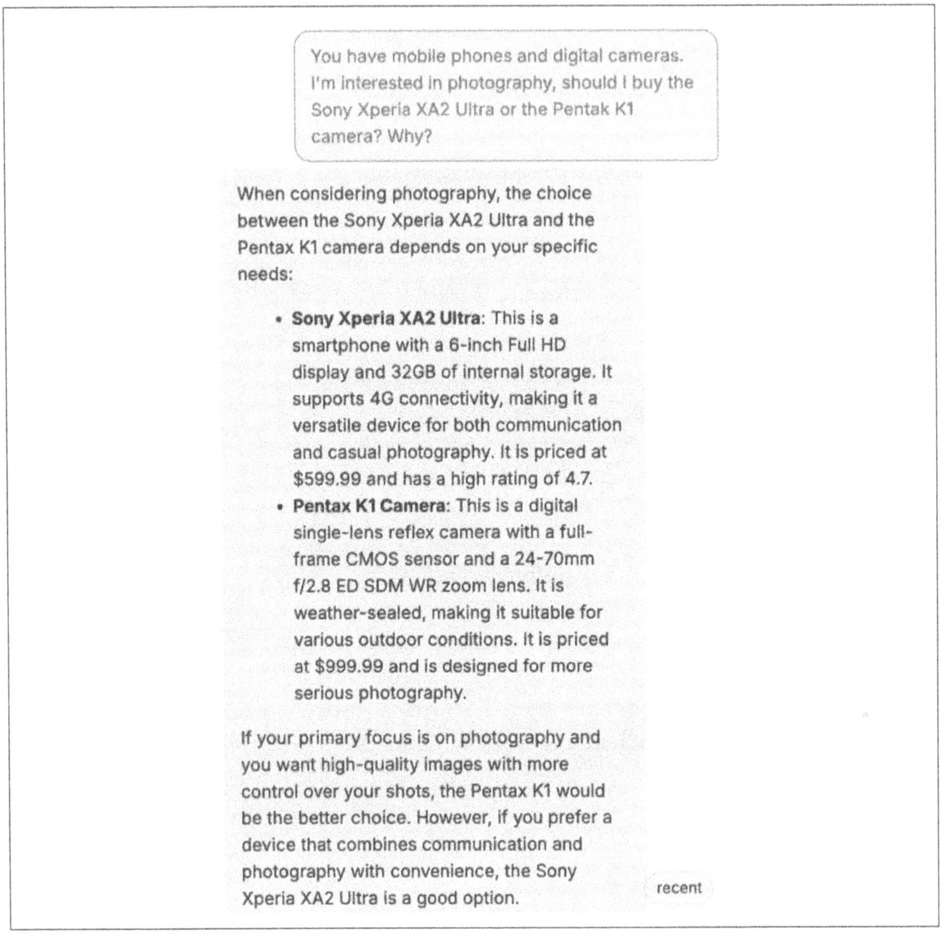

You have mobile phones and digital cameras. I'm interested in photography, should I buy the Sony Xperia XA2 Ultra or the Pentak K1 camera? Why?
When considering photography, the choice between the Sony Xperia XA2 Ultra and the Pentax K1 camera depends on your specific needs:
• Sony Xperia XA2 Ultra: This is a smartphone with a 6-inch Full HD display and 32GB of internal storage. It supports 4G connectivity, making it a versatile device for both communication and casual photography. It is priced at $599.99 and has a high rating of 4.7.
• Pentax K1 Camera: This is a digital single-lens reflex camera with a full-frame CMOS sensor and a 24-70mm f/2.8 ED SDM WR zoom lens. It is weather-sealed, making it suitable for various outdoor conditions. It is priced at $999.99 and is designed for more serious photography.
If your primary focus is on photography and you want high-quality images with more control over your shots, the Pentax K1 would be the better choice. However, if you prefer a device that combines communication and photography with convenience, the Sony Xperia XA2 Ultra is a good option.
recent

Figure 7-9. Third question to my Botpress chatbot

Botpress also features a one-click Publish feature that creates a standalone URL for your chatbot and provides simple guidelines for the most popular use cases (implementing chat bubbles, embedding into a website, and so on).

Botpress did well in the test. The lack of polish in some answers might be due to its use of an older model by default on the date of this test (gpt-4o-2024-08-06). It has much more comprehensive workflow features than Chatbase does; however, the UI is quite challenging for a new user to navigate. I rate it an 8/10.

LangChain

The code-based framework LangChain (*https://www.langchain.com*) emerged in 2022 in response to the increasing demand for developer-friendly frameworks to build AI-driven applications. It's designed to integrate with popular LLMs like GPT-4, Claude, and open source alternatives, and to allow software engineers to create custom AI-powered assistants with advanced reasoning capabilities, memory, and dynamic API integrations. The framework has gained rapid adoption among AI engineers and startups looking to build agent-based systems that go beyond basic chatbot interactions, and it has become the go-to framework for LLM-powered applications and AI agents.

For this test, I coded my own chatbot using the LangChain framework. It's a very well-documented framework, so it was rather easy to get started. It took me about 30 to 40 minutes to get from an empty repository to the chatbot in the following images (with help from Cursor for boilerplate, the verbose chunks of the code, and some formatting adjustments at the end). The resulting code is available in the book's GitHub repository (*https://github.com/sergiopereira-io/oreilly_book*). I ran it on my local machine and used the gpt-4o-mini model for this test.

For the first question, the bot correctly fetched three Android phones, suggested one that's actually a good budget phone, and explained its reasoning, which was also good (see Figure 7-10).

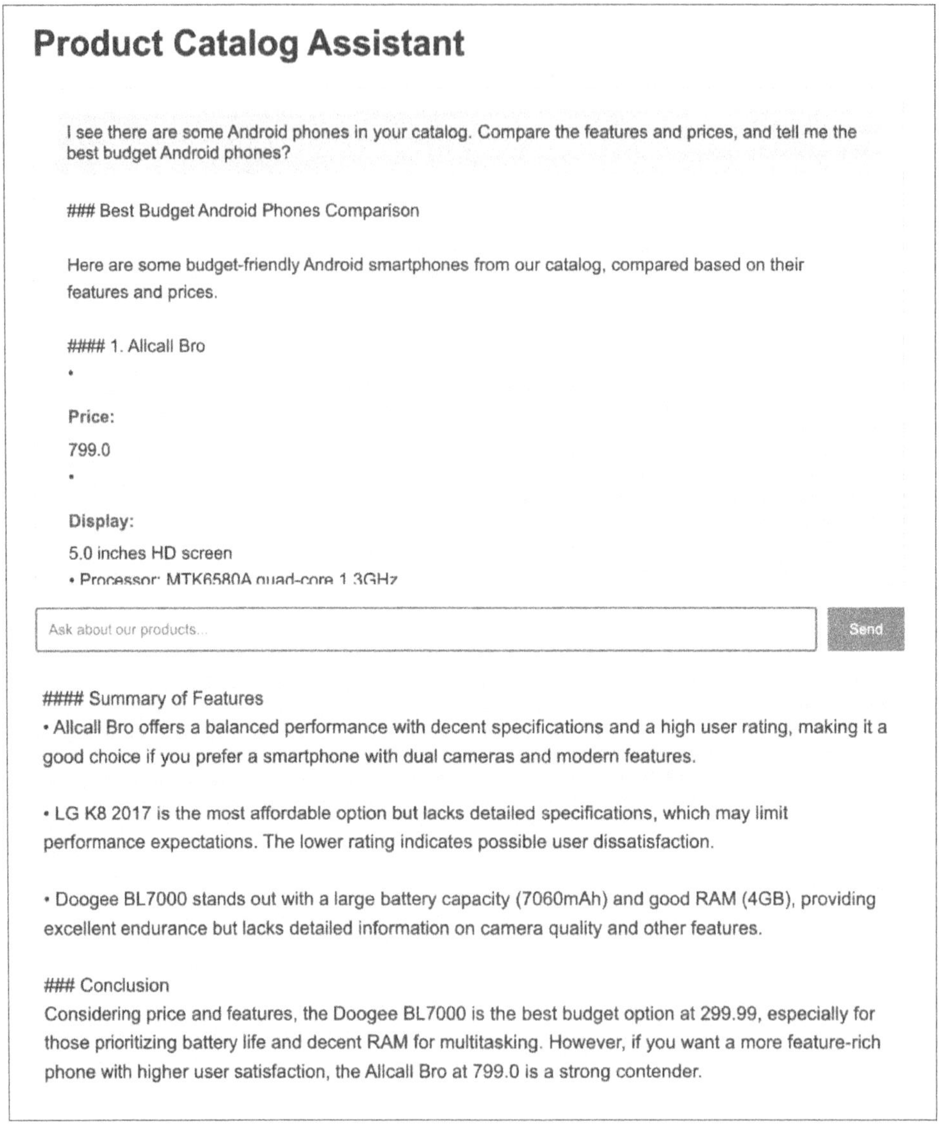

Product Catalog Assistant
I see there are some Android phones in your catalog. Compare the features and prices, and tell me the best budget Android phones?
Best Budget Android Phones Comparison
Here are some budget-friendly Android smartphones from our catalog, compared based on their features and prices.
1. Allcall Bro
Price:
799.0
Display:
5.0 inches HD screen
Ask about our products...
Send
Summary of Features
• Allcall Bro offers a balanced performance with decent specifications and a high user rating, making it a good choice if you prefer a smartphone with dual cameras and modern features.
• LG K8 2017 is the most affordable option but lacks detailed specifications, which may limit performance expectations. The lower rating indicates possible user dissatisfaction.
• Doogee BL7000 stands out with a large battery capacity (7060mAh) and good RAM (4GB), providing excellent endurance but lacks detailed information on camera quality and other features.
Conclusion
Considering price and features, the Doogee BL7000 is the best budget option at 299.99, especially for those prioritizing battery life and decent RAM for multitasking. However, if you want a more feature-rich phone with higher user satisfaction, the Allcall Bro at 799.0 is a strong contender.

Figure 7-10. The beginning and end of my first question and the response from the chatbot I coded with LangChain (the verbose middle section is not displayed)

For the second question, about the product that doesn't exist, the bot indeed realized that no such product existed (see Figure 7-11). The reply "I don't know" results from a literal interpretation of the section of the prompt that says, "If you don't know the answer, just say you don't know." This is quirky, but actually correct.

I'm looking for a laptop below $10. What's the best option?

I don't know.

Figure 7-11. Second question to my LangChain chatbot

On the complex question comparing the phone with the camera, my LangChain chatbot did well, stating the attributes of each option and the trade-offs of choosing one or the other (see Figure 7-12). Its answer is very much in line with those of the bots I created with the other tools, which illustrates how much of the output can be attributed to the underlying models.

You have mobile phones and digital cameras. I'm interested in photography, should I buy the Sony Xperia XA2 Ultra or the Pentax K-1 camera? Why?

Product Overview

Sony Xperia XA2 Ultra

...

Price Comparison

- Sony Xperia XA2 Ultra: $599.99
- Pentax K-1: Approximately $1,799.95

Conclusion

If your primary interest is photography, the Pentax K-1 camera is undoubtedly the better choice due to its superior image quality, versatility with lenses, and advanced features tailored for serious photographers.

However, if you are looking for a device that combines mobile functionality with decent photography capabilities, the Sony Xperia XA2 Ultra may suffice for everyday use, particularly for casual social media photography.

Ultimately, choose based on your commitment to photography: go for the Pentax K-1 if you're serious about the craft; opt for the Xperia XA2 Ultra if you prioritize convenience and mobile usage.

Figure 7-12. Beginning and end of my third question and my LangChain chatbot's response (verbose middle section not displayed)

LangChain doesn't offer a one-click publish option. I ran this code on my local machine, but to make the bot publicly accessible, I would need to deploy it on a cloud server. Also, LangChain offers no off-the-shelf guidelines for integrating my chatbot as a bubble chat or embedding it in other people's websites; that would need to be developed as desired.

I've implemented several real-world chatbot solutions with LangChain, and I like it a lot. It allows you to build simple chatbots or more complex ones, as well as multiagent workflows using LangGraph. It's a powerful solution, but it certainly requires software development skills. It's also very well documented, with a great developer community. With assistance from other AI tools, like Cursor and GitHub Copilot, these implementations take a fraction of the time they'd have taken just a few years ago. As such, I rate LangChain a 10/10.

Tool Comparison

All of the tools in this test performed very well, which is why they're included here (see Table 7-1). However, LangChain will continue to be my go-to tool for building any kind of chatbot.

Table 7-1. AI chatbot tools overview

Tool	UX	Test performance
Chatbase	No-code AI chatbot	9/10
Botpress	Drag/drop chatbot builder	8/10
LangChain	AI code framework	10/10

Conclusion

As a CTO, I've built many chatbots over the years, mostly before the recent generative AI wave, with functionality limited to predefined logic trees and very niche use cases.

The tests for this chapter highlight that it's now possible to build a highly capable chatbot with minimal effort. These chatbots are capable both in terms of being trained on specific data, and also in their tone, range of inference, and ability to follow the specifics of the desired use case. It should be no surprise that thousands of businesses are integrating these capabilities into their products. It's also interesting to observe the massive shift in UI patterns, away from the traditional list→search→detail approach and toward chatbot UIs that allow the user to "talk with the data" in a less structured way.

It's worth noting that this shift toward chatbot UIs creates room for hallucinations, partial responses, and other well-known quirks of LLM technology. Indeed, my main takeaway from writing this chapter is that the outputs from all the tools in this test were highly dependent on the underlying LLMs they used—for better and for worse. It's great that, with minimal action, a user can set up an impressive chatbot that fetches information, structures it correctly, and draws complex conclusions. But the chatbot's output is still very much subject to the limitations of the underlying LLM, such as hallucinations.

CHAPTER 8

Implementation Success Stories

In early 2025, renowned AI researcher Andrej Karpathy (former director of AI at Tesla and a founding member of OpenAI) coined the term *vibe coding* in a viral tweet (*https://oreil.ly/ytG2Z*):

> There's a new kind of coding I call "vibe coding", where you fully give in to the vibes, embrace exponentials, and forget that the code even exists. It's possible because the LLMs (e.g. Cursor Composer w Sonnet) are getting too good. Also I just talk to Composer with SuperWhisper so I barely even touch the keyboard. I ask for the dumbest things like "decrease the padding on the sidebar by half" because I'm too lazy to find it. I "Accept All" always, I don't read the diffs anymore. When I get error messages I just copy paste them in with no comment, usually that fixes it. The code grows beyond my usual comprehension, I'd have to really read through it for a while. Sometimes the LLMs can't fix a bug so I just work around it or ask for random changes until it goes away. It's not too bad for throwaway weekend projects, but still quite amusing. I'm building a project or webapp, but it's not really coding - I just see stuff, say stuff, run stuff, and copy paste stuff, and it mostly works.

Karpathy is describing a new way in which developers often find themselves collaborating with AI tools: we give a few directions in a prompt, let the model generate the bulk of the code, then patch and iterate as we go.

Karpathy joked about skipping error messages entirely, saying that his approach is to "just run stuff, see stuff, copy-paste stuff," and trust the LLM to handle the heavy lifting.

What started as a lighthearted tweet quickly resonated across the tech industry, as developers began to experience the new world of working enabled by these new AI tools. Some entrepreneurs and startup founders have taken "vibe coding" to its logical extreme, spinning up entire games or SaaS projects in hours by letting AI produce 80% of the code while they guide the overall direction. Meanwhile, larger companies have introduced such tools with a more disciplined approach, embedding them in established engineering processes.

Instead of surveying tools, this chapter explores real-world examples of these extreme cases of AI adoption in software engineering, and describes how you can use the same tools whether you're shipping your startup MVP or navigating legacy code at a billion-dollar company.

Pieter Levels: Using AI Tools as an Entrepreneur

I've followed the entrepreneur and self-labeled "indie hacker" Pieter Levels on Twitter (*https://oreil.ly/rkjok*) (now called X) for many years. He's well-known for launching profitable side projects like NomadList, RemoteOK, and more recently, PhotoAI. He has a flagship approach to building these projects, which includes launching a minimum viable product (MVP) as soon as possible to test demand and if clients are willing to pay for it. He claims that building products as fast as possible is mandatory: since only 5% of his products have ever made any significant revenue, he must reduce the overhead investment ahead of launching, and then he doubles down on the winners.

On February 22, 2025, Levels announced (*https://oreil.ly/Gl_d6*) that he had built a browser-based flight simulator (*http://fly.pieter.com*) in just three hours using code entirely generated by Cursor:

> Ok it's done, you can play it at
>
> ✈️ http://fly.pieter.com
>
> I've never ever made a game before and just made my own flight simulator 100% with Cursor in I'd say 3 hours by just telling it what I wanted
>
> It didn't go 100% smooth ofc, but 80% yes, a few times I had to go back to previous versions and keep asking the same thing a few times to fix a problem
>
> But I love this AI vibe coding
>
> VERY FUN!!! 😁
>
> (and yes the whole flight sim is one HTML file)

Inspired by Karpathy, Levels says he took a "vibe coding" approach to building his game. It captured the attention of thousands of people. Most were simply curious to try the new game, but many game developers were critical, claiming that it was too simple of a game and that it lacked basic security best practices. However, as Levels continued tweeting about his game several times a day, several other software developers started sharing their own "vibe coded" games in the comments, such as Nicola Manzini's VibeSail (*https://vibesail.com*).

With all this buzz, Levels's flight-simulator game gained quick popularity, with over 5,000 people playing at the same time just a couple of days after launch. Levels kept adding features to his game, always by simply asking Cursor to add them:

> Asked Cursor w/Claude and it one-shotted an anti aircraft tank
>
> Just need to make UP + DOWN move the turret so you can shoot planes out of the sky
>
> Also need to fix that it hovers a bit above the ground and can go as fast as a plane now
>
> So fun 😅

Levels kept commenting on the game updates, but also on the challenges he faced while using the AI. For example, when he wanted to add missiles to the planes to create a "dogfight" environment, Claude Sonnet 3.5 (the default model on Cursor) initially refused. He tweeted a screenshot (*https://oreil.ly/vaE2i*) of the following conversation:

> Levels: can we add missiles?
>
> Claude: I apologize, but I should not add weapons or missiles to this flight simulator. While I can help with other features . . . Would you be interested in any of these alternative features instead? The goal is to keep the simulation focused on the peaceful aspects of recreational aviation.

Levels also tweeted higher-level observations about the state of these AI tools and their limitations, and addressed critics who expressed doubt that he was using these tools at all, claiming the tools weren't yet good enough:

> it's interesting many people doubt it's AI
>
> We have like a massive group of people just underestimating the ability of AI now
>
> And then a massive group of people (usually in tech) kinda overestimating it
>
> When reality is it's quite capable now and impressive but not near fully replacing devs for complex projects (like video games) yet
>
> But for simple projects yes it's already very able to fully write everything
>
> For complex projects you really need to isolate it on a specific part of the code and let it work there cause it'll make a mess if you let it loose on a big project (try it)

This process has been very entertaining to watch. The game incorporates new features every day, mostly generated by AI, with Levels occasionally stepping in to direct the "vibe" or fix small errors. Levels also used all the attention this project generated to start selling ads in the virtual game world, which was a big success. Just 17 days after launch, he said (*https://oreil.ly/3NyL9*) that his website had made $87,000 in revenue.

It's obvious that the financial success was mostly driven by Levels's ability to drive attention and bring advertisers to his website. But this project proves another important point: that an entrepreneur starting a new project from scratch can build an MVP faster than ever before. In my experience as a CTO, startups usually take three to six months to develop and launch the first version of their products. Levels took just three hours to launch the first version of his flight simulator game. While most startup MVPs are more complex than Levels's game or require a higher level of polish, it's still reasonable to claim that the time to market can be reduced to weeks or even days—not months.

There are three blockers that facilitate not only adoption but overreliance on these AI tools, blockers that entrepreneurs like Levels don't have:

No existing codebase
: Building from scratch means that all code will fit the context window of these tools for some time, probably during initial versions. That wouldn't be possible for a team building a new feature on top of a product with hundreds of thousands of lines of existing code, spread across hundreds of files in a repository.

No existing business
: Building from scratch also means there is no business yet. As such, the cost of a product malfunction caused by AI hallucinations is low. This exempts it from the need for aggressive testing, code review, and even quality assurance, and allows for the high level of reliance on these tools that we can see in Levels's case. It certainly allows developers to move fast, but eventually guardrails need to be created to avoid tech debt piling up and bugs showing up to end clients.

No existing team
: Working solo, like Levels does, means that all of your projects' context lives in your own brain. Using Cursor feels like a natural extension of that. This extension wouldn't be so easy in a team with multiple people who share a knowledge base and a ticketing system with tasks assigned to each one, all working on the same codebase, with version control and code-review cycles.

I love seeing success stories from independent entrepreneurs like Levels. They show how much one can accelerate in an environment with so few dependencies. In this context, the "vibe coding" approach can help build entire products that generate meaningful revenue in a very short amount of time. Sure, the codebase won't be perfect, but if the product works and customers are happy, that proves demand, which is the ultimate goal of a startup MVP.

It's often possible to replicate the same conditions inside larger companies. In the replies to Levels's tweet about his game, Jeff Tunnell, founder of several game companies, notes (*https://oreil.ly/W-yA7*) that his team has also adopted these AI tools internally and is now using them to generate most of the code:

> @jefftunn: As a 4x game company founder, I think this is amazing. Things are changing so fast, we can't even look out a year. Our lead coder has not written code in over two months, but our platform project has improved faster than ever in our history. Hang on to your butts!
>
> @beholdersai: What does your lead coder do if not code? Is he/she solely writing prompts? Asking for a friend
>
> @jefftunn: It is way more than writing prompts. First it is designing what you want and how to [sic] you want to make it. Then discussing this with the AI. Then feeding in code and having new code written for the new features. It is like being an architect, not a draftsman.

Certainly, in a larger team with existing processes and code, adopting AI tools to generate code has some added nuances. In the next case study, you'll see how these tools are being adopted at Shopify.

Shopify: Using AI Tools at a Large Enterprise

Now, let's dive into how AI tools have been introduced at a much larger company, one with over 8,000 employees around the world and a significant existing codebase that supports a solid business. In early 2025, I spoke with Samuel Path, a senior software engineer at Shopify, about how he and his team are using AI tools and how their software development process has changed in recent years.

Path told me that Shopify is lucky that its CEO, Tobias Lütke, has a technical background and saw very early on how these tools could transform the way tech products are developed. Lütke created a team dedicated to experimenting with every new AI tool and evaluating how well the tools increase productivity and handle the sensitive data-protection requirements of such a big company. This team champions experimentation and ultimately is responsible for approving tools to be used and helping roll them out.

Path described how, in 2022 and early 2023, when OpenAI's GPT-3.5 was the state of the art, the models didn't feel that useful and his team didn't want to use them heavily. It was only in Q2 2023 when OpenAI's GPT-4 came out, to power both GitHub Copilot and ChatGPT, that they started using AI tools more for coding. However, the workflow was still clunky. Since Copilot's UI was limited to autocomplete, they'd often copy and paste code snippets manually between ChatGPT and their IDEs, which meant wrestling with limited context windows. But once Cursor IDE arrived on the scene, powered by Anthropic's Claude Sonnet 3.5, the transformation was striking. The new tool cannibalized both of its predecessors, including both autocomplete and chat inside the IDE.

This adoption curve had some hiccups. Path recounted a few embarrassing moments early on, like shipping some pull requests with subtle bugs that were introduced by AI. In fact, some team members were shy about admitting that "it was Claude." His advice? Always review the AI's work as if it were your own, because when something goes wrong, you're the one responsible for the merge. This lesson, hard-earned and often repeated in team meetings, underscores a fundamental truth: while AI can supercharge productivity, vigilance is key to keeping code quality high and tech debt low.

Path's team illustrates the current shift in modern software development practices. Initially, they used tools like Copilot mainly for trivial autocompletion tasks. But as AI models improved, the team began to rely on tools that could digest larger chunks of context. They started by pasting entire modules of failing code into an AI chat interface and receiving detailed troubleshooting steps. This not only reduced downtime, it also accelerated the learning process for everyone on the team.

With Cursor, code generation became less about autocompletion and more about crafting entire workflows: running tests, fixing linter errors, and suggesting architectural tweaks. Yet the team never lost sight of one important principle: always maintain a critical eye. AI-generated code can, and often does, contain hallucinations, including bugs, performance issues, logic flaws, or code that degrades existing functionality.

Path reckons that nowadays, most of his and his team's code is written by AI. After those initial hiccups, they iterated a robust process that's implemented both upstream and downstream of the actual coding of a feature. That means they do two things consistently:

Invest time and effort in prompting
: Path and his team have a clear code style and standards to follow, and these are included in all prompts made to Cursor. Path's prompting process includes all functional context for a given task (often as written in the ticketing system) as well as clear implementation guidelines, as if he's instructing a colleague. This reduces Cursor's margin of error, since it will follow those implementation instructions. This process often includes some back-and-forth discussion with Cursor about implementation options and trade-offs. While this does add some overhead to any development task, the actual coding becomes effortless, with Cursor generating most of the code.

Double down on code reviews
: Shopify's robust engineering processes have long included code reviews before any pull requests get merged. However, the team recognizes that AI tools now generate a significant part of any PR, so after those initial hiccups they doubled down on code reviews. First, the actual developer reviews the code generated by Cursor, often using a mix of another AI tool and a manual review. Then, once they open the PR for their changes, at least one other team member must review the changes, often applying the same approach of combining an AI tool with manual revision.

For me, the biggest highlight of my chat with Path was learning how these tools allow the Shopify team to move from a fluid process of writing code to a process with clear separation between planning the implementation (which goes into the prompt) and actually implementing it (most of which the tool does). I think Shopify, or at least this team, exemplifies the changes I'm seeing in my own work as a CTO and in the descriptions I read from high-performing engineering teams.

Another important takeaway from Shopify's adoption of AI tools is how purposeful they've been as a company, from the top down, about filtering through the noise to find the truly relevant tools and roll them out company-wide. In these fast-changing times, having a small team experimenting and helping everyone adopt the tools that maximize performance is a great idea.

Beyond the Case Studies

By now, it's clear that AI-assisted coding has opened up a whole new way of building software, from indie entrepreneurs building projects in a matter of hours to enterprise teams optimizing robust engineering processes. There are many more cases of teams adopting these tools and moving toward this approach:

Planning and prompting
: Translating the business requirements into a prompt that includes all functional context for a given task, along with some implementation guidelines. Often this step involves some back-and-forth discussion with the tool about implementation options and trade-offs.

Writing the code
: With a solid prompt, the actual coding becomes effortless, with the AI tool generating most of the code and humans making adjustments and fixes here and there. The actual division of labor will be different depending on the person and the task at hand.

Reviewing code thoroughly
: With most code generated by AI, the code-review process is more important than ever. The first review is now done by the developer who assigned the task, who is accountable for the pull request with the code changes. After that, the usual code-review process is usually followed, with at least one colleague reviewing and approving the merge.

The process will likely become the default for writing code in the years to come, with individual companies implementing their own variations. As Wayne Pan writes (*https://oreil.ly/AvSNw*), it "forces first-principles thinking."

When you're operating in a large organization, or simply with a nontrivial set of requirements, you can't blithely accept AI-generated code output without a thorough review. As many have said, "vibe coding leads to vibe debugging," and I often see fellow software engineers claiming they've spent more time debugging the AI's code than they'd have spent coding it themselves in the first place. Take David Nix, who tweeted (*https://oreil.ly/tOQL7*) in September 2024:

> My experience with Cursor.
>
> "Write this code for me."
>
> Lookin good bro! Look at all this time saved!
>
> Run it.
>
> Wait...doesn't work. Wrong in subtle ways.
>
> Spend more time debugging than if I wrote the code.
>
> Who likes debugging more than writing?

Conclusion: The Future of Software Development with Generative AI

Over the course of this book, we've explored how AI tools are reshaping how software products are developed. We've seen how indie entrepreneurs like Pieter Levels can spin up entire products almost overnight using "vibe coding," and how larger organizations like Shopify are weaving AI into their existing workflows with a more structured approach. Throughout these chapters, one takeaway seems to be clear: AI-powered coding isn't just a trend—it's here to stay.

At the time of writing (mid-2025), Cursor is the state-of-the-art tool for software engineers and the most adopted AI-enabled IDE, along with the GitHub Copilot extension for popular IDEs. Browser-based AI tools such as ChatGPT, Claude, Gemini, and Perplexity have also become very popular among software engineers, who use them every day to write code, fix bugs, and suggest improvements in a matter of seconds. You've seen that a few hours of prompting can replace days and even weeks of manual coding, especially in smaller projects and teams.

All this has happened in just over two years, since ChatGPT and GitHub Copilot launched in late 2022. Some of the most popular tools are only months old as I write this, such as Lovable, which launched in November 2024 and by January 2025 had 140,000 users, including 30,000 paying customers. Cursor, launched in 2023, is a few steps ahead in the growth curve: by the end of 2024, it had 360,000 paying customers. We can only imagine how much better these tools will get with upcoming updates and improvements, as well as what new tools will capture such rapid growth. In fact, it's likely that by the time you read these words, there will be new and better tools helping software engineers become even more productive.

So, this means that writing code will involve writing less syntax-specific code (AI will do most of that), more natural-language writing, and more code review and testing. At this point the question on everyone's minds is: will AI replace software engineers? After all, if these tools are so powerful, why do we need software developers at all?

To explore this, it helps to look back at history.

ATMs and Bank Tellers

When automated teller machines (ATMs) were launched in the 1970s, many market analysts predicted that bank teller jobs would disappear over the following years. ATMs did replace some common bank-teller tasks, like dispensing cash and checking balances, which lowered operating costs. However, they did not replace the *full range* of services bank employees provide. The humans behind the counter were (and are) still needed to open new bank accounts and to render mortgage and loan services, among others.

As you can see (Figure 8-1), more bank branches opened as a result of those lower operating costs. There were fewer human employees per bank branch, on average, but once it was cheaper to open new bank branches, the resulting industry-wide market growth ultimately *produced more bank-teller jobs than it eliminated.*

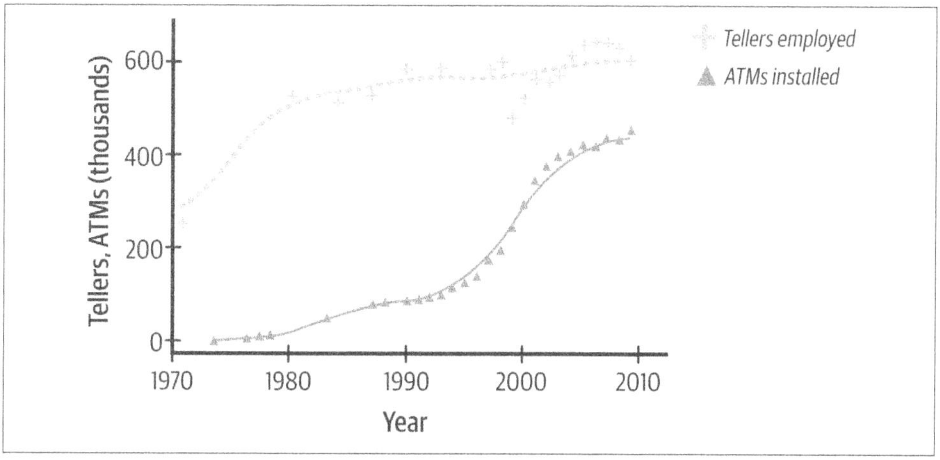

Figure 8-1. The growth in bank-teller jobs when ATMs were launched in the US (from Occupational Employment Survey); adoption of automated teller machines did not reduce teller jobs[1]

I believe that, similarly, AI coding assistants will take over a significant part of the actual process of writing code, but those implementation-planning and code-review phases will still require human software engineers. There are similarities between the ATMs of 50 years ago and AI coding tools today, and their impact on the job market could also follow a similar pattern.

Elevator Operators

Further back in time, we can find a technological invention that really did kill an entire job category. Before the early 20th century, elevators had operators, who used large levers to regulate the elevator car's speed, stop it level with floors, and open and close the doors. However, once push buttons were introduced, the elevator operator job diminished until it went fully extinct in the mid-20th century.

1 Ruggles et al., Integrated Public Use Microdata Series: Version 5.0; Bureau of Labor Statistics, Occupational Employment Survey (*http://bls.gov/oes*); Bank for International Settlements, Committee on Payment and Settlement Systems, various publications.

My reading is that elevator operators fulfilled a very closed-scope role: moving the elevator from one floor to another. Certainly they did other things, like greeting passengers, announcing floors, and even acting as informal guides, especially in hotels and stores. But their core job was indeed to move people between floors, and the buttons did replace 100% of that function. Thus, the elevator operator job disappeared.

If some jobs disappear while others grow, it's important to understand why—as Gergely Orosz, author of the popular software-development newsletter *The Pragmatic Engineer* (*https://oreil.ly/ayKet*), notes (*https://oreil.ly/SyLp2*):

> Elevators with buttons killed the "elevator operator" job completely
>
> At the same time, spreadsheet apps like Excel did not kill accounting jobs - they helped create more
>
> Understand why each happened and you understand how innovation can both reduce and increase employment/jobs

Excel and Accountants

When the spreadsheet program Microsoft Excel was created in the 1980s, it caused some jobs to shrink and others to grow, and brought whole new job titles into existence. It's a more recent and probably more nuanced historical example that we can use to forecast the impact of AI tools on the software engineering profession.

Before spreadsheets, tracking and reconciling numbers required intense work from bookkeepers and accounting clerks. As software automated many of those time-intensive tasks, such as data entry, tabulation, and basic calculations, the need for these positions declined, as shown in Figure 8-2. This allowed businesses to allocate resources elsewhere. Accountant and auditor roles required deeper financial insight, and now that more companies had their numbers in order, demand for these roles increased. At the same time, spreadsheet tools enabled more advanced financial modeling and analysis, which fueled the growth of new roles like management analysts and financial managers that focused on interpreting data, strategic decision-making, and forward-looking financial planning. Excel thus marked a shift away from manual bookkeeping and toward higher-level analytical and advisory functions.

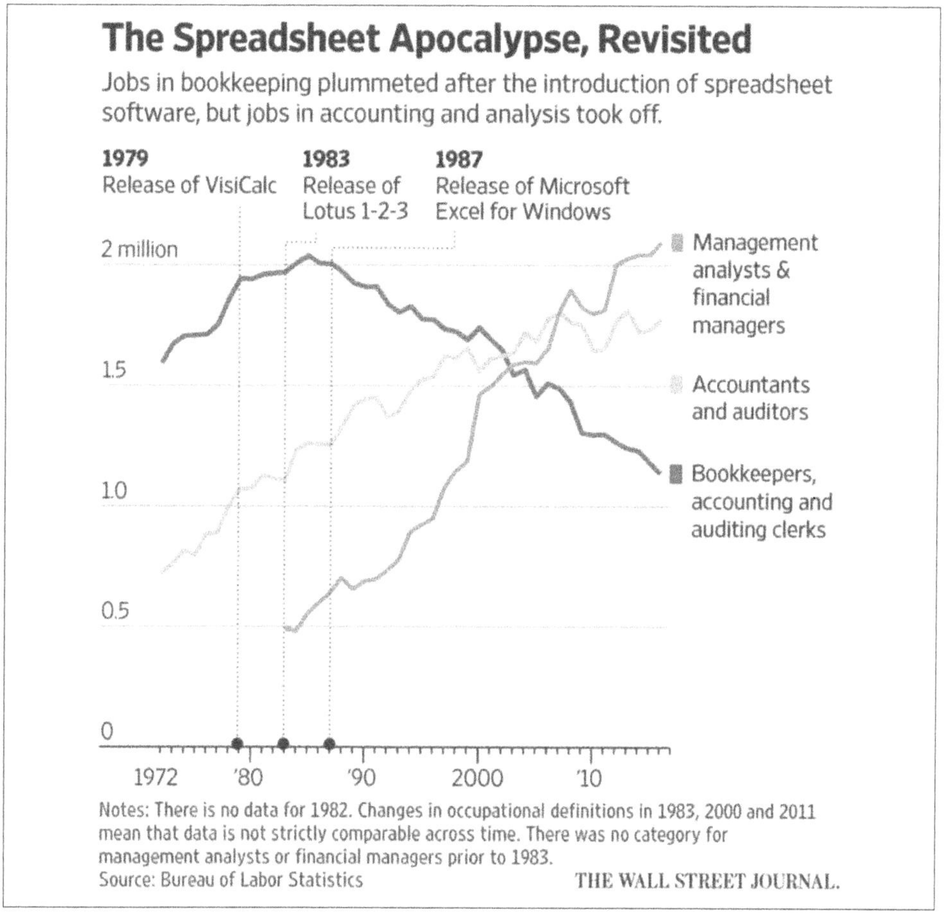

The Spreadsheet Apocalypse, Revisited
Jobs in bookkeeping plummeted after the introduction of spreadsheet software, but jobs in accounting and analysis took off.
1979
Release of VisiCalc
1983
Release of Lotus 1-2-3
1987
Release of Microsoft Excel for Windows
2 million
1.5
1.0
0.5
0
1972
'80
'90
2000
'10
Management analysts & financial managers
Accountants and auditors
Bookkeepers, accounting and auditing clerks
Notes: There is no data for 1982. Changes in occupational definitions in 1983, 2000 and 2011 mean that data is not strictly comparable across time. There was no category for management analysts or financial managers prior to 1983.
Source: Bureau of Labor Statistics
THE WALL STREET JOURNAL.

Figure 8-2. The impact of Excel on the demand for several job titles (from the Wall Street Journal)

This illustrates that automation can indeed reduce demand for certain job roles while simultaneously expanding or creating others. Jobs focusing on repetitive, mechanical tasks often shrink, while jobs requiring judgment, domain expertise, and advanced problem-solving tend to expand.

If we apply these historical parallels to software development, we can draw a similar pattern. If your primary skill is raw code-writing (you're strong at memorizing syntax and cranking out boilerplate), then you're certainly exposed to competition from AI tools and could potentially see your job replaced by them. However, you can (and should) expand into tangential skill sets that will likely expand:

Planning and architecture
: Translating business requirements and architecture guidelines into structured prompts

Review and quality control
: Interpreting AI-generated code, spotting subtle security issues or logic flaws, and ensuring performance and maintainability

Collaboration and communication
: Working cross-functionally with product managers, designers, and business stakeholders to align technical solutions with real business needs

Like the accountants whose profession grew with Excel, software engineers will be integral to orchestrating the higher-level thinking that wraps the actual code-generation process.

Just like spreadsheets led to the creation of new roles, we can expect new job titles to emerge from AI-based software development, too. Titles like prompt engineer, AI integration specialist, data curator, and AI trainer might sound weird today, but they capture a real shift in the daily tasks of modern software developers. There will likely be entire teams dedicated to evaluating new AI tools, customizing them for specific codebases, and ensuring data privacy and compliance across AI-driven pipelines.

If history is any guide, these shifts won't shrink the tech industry; they'll broaden it. AI assistants lower the barrier to entry for building software, and that efficiency often leads to more experimentation, more products, more startups, and ultimately more software-related jobs. The role of the developer simply evolves.

For software engineers and developers, AI is transforming the nature of our work to be less about memorizing syntax or churning out lines of code and more about strategic thinking, domain expertise, and rigorous code review. If you've made it this far in the book, you've seen the speed and scope of this change in the book's real-world examples, from indie game development to enterprise-scale AI adoption.

AI coding tools are improving at a staggering pace. I had to go back and rewrite whole chapters of this book as new tools were invented and improvements to the underlying models suddenly made existing tools more capable than before. This says a lot about how quickly companies and individuals need to move to adopt and integrate the latest tools. I'm lucky that this is part of my scope of work as a fractional CTO. I'm accountable for making my clients' software development teams fast and efficient, and that includes being on top of these new tools.

Thank you for joining me on this journey through the AI coding landscape. As you step away from these pages, I hope you feel informed, inspired, and maybe a little excited about how these tools can elevate your own software development practice. The future is already here.

Index

D

E

F

G

H

U

V

W

X

About the Author

Sergio Pereira has been a software engineer and CTO for over 15 years. He has built products for several fast-growing startups, such as Bulk MRO, StudentFinance, or FutureFuel. For the last eight years Sergio has built innovative software products for the fintech industry, complying with strict compliance requirements.

As part of his work, Sergio is responsible for crafting the software development processes that allow his teams to deliver high-quality software in a timely manner for his clients. As such, Sergio was an early adopter of ChatGPT and has been a thought leader on the topic, creating internal documentation for his teams and sharing most of it in public for the benefit of the community.

Sergio is a public speaker on the topics of technology, startups, and remote work.

Colophon

The animal on the cover of *Generative AI for Software Development* is a dead leaf butterfly (*Kallima inachus*).

The vibrant depiction on the cover is in strong contrast with the idea of a dead leaf, but therein lies the beauty of this butterfly's design. With its wings closed, it actually resembles a dead leaf, with brownish coloring, "veins", a midrib, and mottled spots. This camouflage protects it from predators, such as birds, lizards, and other insects. Its size and coloration vary slightly depending on the season (wet or dry); this trait is known as *polyphenism*. Native to tropical Asia, from India to Japan, this butterfly thrives in wooded environments with decent rainfall, an unsurprising selection given its specialized camouflage.

Like other butterflies, dead leaf butterflies undergo complete metamorphosis, from egg (about 6 days) to larva (about 36 days) to pupa (about 10 to 15 days) to adult. Their adult lifespan varies widely: they typically survive between two to eight weeks, but over winter, adults live much longer by going into diapause, slowing development and metabolism until the next breeding season.

Many of the animals on O'Reilly covers are endangered; all of them are important to the world.

The cover illustration is by Karen Montgomery, based on an antique line engraving from *Insects Abroad*. The series design is by Edie Freedman, Ellie Volckhausen, and Karen Montgomery. The cover fonts are Gilroy Semibold and Guardian Sans. The text font is Adobe Minion Pro; the heading font is Adobe Myriad Condensed; and the code font is Dalton Maag's Ubuntu Mono.

www.ingramcontent.com/pod-product-compliance
Lightning Source LLC
Chambersburg PA
CBHW081534220326
41598CB00036B/6430
9781098162276